Dramascripts

The Diary of Anne Frank

Dramatised by
FRANCES GOODRICH & ALBERT HACKETT

*With explanatory notes
and activities by*
JOHN O'CONNOR

Nelson

Thomas Nelson & Sons Ltd
Nelson House
Mayfield Road
Walton-on-Thames
Surrey KT12 5PL
United Kingdom

The Diary of Anne Frank - the script
© Albert Hackett, Francis Goodrich Hackett and Otto Frank 1956
The right of Albert Hackett, Francis Goodrich Hackett and Otto Frank to be identified as authors of this play has been asserted by Michael Joseph Ltd in accordance with Copyright, Design and Patents Act 1988.

Introduction, activities and explanatory notes by John O'Connor
© Thomas Nelson 1998

Designed and produced by Bender Richardson White
Typesetting by Malcolm Smythe
Cover illustration by Dave Grimwood
Black and white illustrations by John James
Printed in Croatia by Zrinski

This edition published by Thomas Nelson & Sons Ltd 1998
ISBN 0 - 17 - 432550 - 9
9 8 7 6 5 4 3
03 04 05 06 07

CONTENTS

Series editor's introduction   iv

Introduction   v

The Characters   viii

THE DIARY OF ANNE FRANK

ACT 1

Scene 1   1

Scene 2   6

Scene 3   21

Scene 4   48

Scene 5   56

ACT 2

Scene 1   71

Scene 2   86

Scene 3   97

Scene 4   108

Scene 5   114

Extracts from the original diary of Anne Frank   116

Looking Back at the Play   119

SERIES EDITOR'S INTRODUCTION

Dramascripts is an exciting series of plays especially chosen for students in the lower and middle years of secondary school. The titles range from the best in modern writing to adaptations of classic texts such as *A Christmas Carol* and *Silas Marner*.

Dramascripts can be read or acted purely for the enjoyment and stimulation that they provide; however, each play in the series also offers all the support that pupils need in working with the text in the classroom:

- **Introduction** – this offers important background information and explains something about the ways in which the play came to be written.
- **Script** – this is clearly set out in ways that make the play easy to handle in the classroom.
- **Notes** explain references that pupils might not understand, and language points that are not obvious.
- **Activities** – at the end of scenes, acts or sections – give pupils the opportunity to explore the play more fully. Types of activity include: discussion, writing, hot-seating, improvisation, interviewing, acting, freeze-framing, story-boarding and artwork.
- **Looking Back at the Play** – this section has further activities for more extended work on the play as a whole with emphasis on characters, plots, themes and language.

THE DIARY OF ANNE FRANK

Anne Frank was only thirteen when, in 1942, she and her family (her mother, father and sister) went into hiding from the Nazis in the sealed-off upper rooms of an office building in Amsterdam, Holland.

Her parents, who were German Jews, had fled from their native land to Holland after Adolf Hitler had come to power in 1933. Hitler hated the Jews and blamed them for everything. At first he tried to force them to emigrate, but by 1941 the decision was taken to carry out the 'final solution' of the Jewish problem – total extermination. Jews were forced to wear a yellow star and restrictions were imposed preventing them from riding bicycles, travelling by tram or even sitting in the garden after eight o'clock in the evening. Many Jews escaped to neighbouring countries, the

Western Europe in 1940 highlighting Nazi-occupied land.

V

Franks among them. But the Franks were not to know that, by 1940, Holland would be in Nazi hands, or that millions of Jews were to die in the concentration camps.

When the Nazis in Holland began to round up Dutch Jews and send them to the death camps, Otto Frank and his family did what thousands of other Jews had done. Leaving behind false evidence that they had fled to Switzerland, they hid themselves away in the hope that the Nazis would one day be defeated. In hiding with them – in a sealed-off room up a small flight of stairs behind a bookcase in an Amsterdam warehouse – were a family of Dutch Jews, the Van Daans, and later, a dentist called Jan Dussel. Each day of their self-imposed imprisonment, they would receive food and other necessities from non-Jewish friends, but they never set foot outside the building for fear of being spotted.

In August, 1944 – after two years in hiding – they were betrayed to the Gestapo and taken to concentration camps. Of the nine who had hidden, only Anne's father, Otto Frank, was to survive. Anne herself died of typhus in the appalling conditions of the concentration camp at Belsen, only two months before Holland was freed from Nazi rule and three months before what would have been her sixteenth birthday.

Miep Gees, the young Dutch girl who had helped the Franks, visited their hiding place a few days after their arrest. This is what she wrote:

'It was terrible, when I went up there. Not a soul in the place. The rooms suddenly looked so big. Everything had been turned upside-down and rummaged through. On the floor lay clothes, papers, letters and school notebooks. Anne's little wrap hung from a hook on the wall. I took it with me. And among the papers on the floor lay a notebook with a checked red cover. I picked it up, looked at the pages and recognised Anne's handwriting.'

The notebook was, of course, Anne's diary: a remarkable document which records not only Anne's optimism, but also her understanding of relationships, love, fear and loneliness. At one point she writes, *'I still believe that people are really good at heart.'*

Anne's diary has been translated into thirty languages. The play version, written in 1956, has been seen in as many countries and has also been made into a film.

It is difficult to turn a diary into a stage play. For one thing, the diary is obviously told from Anne's point of view, whereas in the play, she is one of the characters. For another, the diary is full of impressions and ideas, but in a play, these have to be represented by incidents in a story that can be performed by actors. But the authors visited the building in Amsterdam, talked to Otto Frank, Anne's father, and finally, after eight drafts, produced what one critic called 'one of the most astonishing documents of the war'.

This presents one interpretation of how the set of the play The Diary of Anne Frank *might look. Compare with the stage directions at the beginning of Act, Scene 1 on page 1.*

THE CHARACTERS

THE FRANK FAMILY:

MR OTTO FRANK a business-man in his 40s. Anne calls him Pim.

MRS EDITH FRANK his wife, younger than her husband.

MARGOT their eighteen-year-old daughter.

ANNE their thirteen-year-old daughter, also sometimes called Anneke and Anneline.

THE VAN DAAN FAMILY:

MR VAN DAAN a man in his late 40s. His wife calls him Putti.

MRS PETRONELLA VAN DAAN his wife, in her early 40s. Her husband calls her Kerli.

PETER their sixteen-year-old son.

THE DUTCH HELPERS:

MIEP GEES nineteen when she helps the Franks move into the attic. Sometimes called Miepia.

MR KRALER middle-aged.

THE EXTRA GUEST:

MR JAN DUSSEL a dentist, late 50s.

Pronouncing the names

Many names (such as Frank) can be pronounced almost as if they were English and you won't be far out. Some are harder, however. Miep Gees is pronounced *meep geese* and Kraler is *krah-ler* (the *ah* is like the vowel sound in *barn*). Although it is usual to pronounce Anne in the English way, it is actually *ah-ne* (the final –*e* like the vowel sound in *let*). Her other pet names, Anneke and Anneline are pronounced *ah-ne-ke* and *ah-ne-lee-ne*. The dentist is *yan doo-sell* (the *oo* like the vowel sound in *book*).

THE DIARY OF ANNE FRANK
ACT 1 ❖ SCENE 1

The scene remains the same throughout the play. It is the top floor of a warehouse and office building in Amsterdam, Holland. The sharply peaked roof of the building is outlined against a sea of other roof-tops, stretching away into the distance. Nearby is the belfry of a church tower, the Westertoren, whose carillon rings out the hours. Occasionally faint sounds float up from below: the voices of children playing in the street, the tramp of marching fee, a boat whistle from the canal.

   The three rooms of the top floor and a small attic space above are exposed to our view. The largest of the rooms is in the centre, with two small rooms, slightly raised, on either side. On the right is a bathroom, out of sight. A narrow steep flight of stairs at the back leads up to the attic. The rooms are sparsely furnished with a few chairs, cots, a table or two. The windows are painted over, or covered with makeshift blackout curtains. In the main room there is a sink, a gas ring for cooking and a wood-burning stove for warmth.

   The room on the left is hardly more than a cupboard. There is a skylight in the sloping ceiling. Directly under this room is a small steep stair-well, with steps leading down to a door. This is the only entrance from the building below. When the door is opened we see that it has been concealed on the outer side by a bookcase attached to it.

Amsterdam, Holland *Amsterdam is one of the main cities in Holland (the Netherlands), a country which had been occupied by the Nazis for most of the war.*

Westertoren *The local church. Its bells are heard at times throughout the play.*

carillon *A peal of bells, worked mechanically.*

blackout curtains *As in Great Britain, all buildings were required to put up blackout curtains or make some arrangements to ensure that no light from indoors could be seen by enemy planes.*

The curtain rises on an empty stage. It is late afternoon November, 1945.

The rooms are dusty, the curtains in rags. Chairs and tables are overturned.

The door at the foot of the small stair-well swings open. MR FRANK comes up the steps into view. He is a gentle, cultured European in his middle years. There is still a trace of a German accent in his speech.

He stands looking slowly around, making a supreme effort at self-control. He is weak, ill. His clothes are threadbare.

After a second he drops his rucksack on the couch and moves slowly about. He opens the door to one of the smaller rooms, and then abruptly closes it again, turning away. He goes to the window at the back, looking off at the Westertoren as its carillon strikes the hour of six, then he moves restlessly on.

From the street below we hear the sound of a barrel organ and children's voices at play. There is a many-coloured scarf hanging from a nail. MR FRANK takes it, putting it around his neck. As he starts for his rucksack, his eye is caught by something lying on the floor. It is a woman's white glove. He holds it in his hand and suddenly all of his self-control is gone. He breaks down, crying.

We hear footsteps on the stairs. MIEP GIES comes up, looking for MR FRANK. MIEP is a Dutch girl of about twenty-two. She wears a coat and hat, ready to go home. She is pregnant. Her attitude toward MR FRANK is protective, compassionate.

MIEP	Are you all right, Mr Frank?	1
MR FRANK	*(Quickly controlling himself.)* Yes, Miep, yes.	
MIEP	Everyone in the office has gone home . . . it's after six. *(Then pleading.)* Don't stay up here, Mr Frank. What's the use of torturing yourself like this?	
MR FRANK	I've come to say good-bye . . . I'm leaving here, Miep.	

November 1945 *The war had ended in May, but it took many people some time to return to their homes, especially if, like Mr Frank, they had been imprisoned in another country.*

a trace of a German accent *Anne's parents were German and had come to live in Holland in 1933.*

MIEP GIES . . . and Mr Kraler *Miep Gies and Mr Kraler hid the family during the war and brought them food, clothes, books and other supplies.*

MIEP	What do you mean? Where are you going? Where?
MR FRANK	I don't know yet. I haven't decided.
MIEP	Mr Frank, you can't leave here. This is your home! Amsterdam is your home. Your business is here, waiting for you . . . You're needed here . . . Now that the war is over, there are things that . . .
MR FRANK	I can't stay in Amsterdam, Miep. It has too many memories for me. Everywhere there's something,. . . the house we lived in . . . the school . . . that street organ playing out there . . . I'm not the person you used to know Miep. I'm a bitter old man. *(Breaking off.)* Forgive me. I shouldn't speak to you like this . . . after all that you did for us . . . the suffering . . .
MIEP	No. No. It wasn't suffering. You can't say we suffered.
	(As she speaks, she straightens a chair which is overturned.)
MR FRANK	I know what you went through, you and Mr Kraler. I'll remember it as long as I live. *(He gives one last look around.)* Come, Miep.
	(He starts for the steps, then remembers his rucksack, going back to get it.)
MIEP	*(Hurrying up to a cupboard.)* Mr Frank, did you see? There are some of your papers here. *(She brings a bundle of papers to him.)* We found them in a heap of rubbish on the floor after . . . after you left.
MR FRANK	Burn them.
	(He opens his rucksack to put the glove in it.)
MIEP	But, Mr Frank, there are letters, notes . . .
MR FRANK	Burn them. All of them.
MIEP	Burn *this?*
	(She hands him a paperbound notebook.)

10

20

30

3

MR FRANK	*(Quietly.)* Anne's diary. *(He opens the diary and begins to read.)* 'Monday, the sixth of July, nineteen forty-two.' *(To MIEP.)* Nineteen forty-two. Is it possible, Miep? . . . Only three years ago. *(As he continues his reading, he sits down on the* **40** *couch.)* 'Dear Diary, since you and I are going to be great friends, I will start by telling you about myself. My name is Anne Frank. I am thirteen years old. I was born in Germany the twelfth of June, nineteen twenty-nine. As my family is Jewish, we emigrated to Holland when Hitler came to power.'
	(As MR FRANK reads on, another voice joins his, as if coming from the air. It is Anne's voice.)
MR FRANK AND ANNE'S VOICE	'My father started a business, importing spice and herbs. Things went well for us until nineteen forty. Then the war **50** came, and the Dutch capitulation, followed by the arrival of the Germans. Then things got very bad for the Jews.'
	(MR FRANK'S voice dies out. ANNE'S VOICE continues alone. The lights dim slowly to darkness. The curtain falls on the scene.)
ANNE'S VOICE	You could not do this and you could not do that. They forced Father out of his business. We had to wear yellow stars. I had to turn in my bike. I couldn't go to a Dutch school any more. I couldn't go to the cinema, or ride in a motor car, or even on a streetcar, and a million other **60**

As my family is Jewish, we emigrated to Holland when Hitler came to power. *Hitler became Chancellor of Germany in January, 1933. As it was clear that he and his Nazi party had a hatred of Jews and would treat them very badly, many Jewish families thought that they could escape the persecutions by emigrating to neighbouring countries. They could not have known that the Nazis were to invade and occupy those countries within a few years, nor could they have foreseen how severe the persecutions would become.*

Dutch capitulation *Holland 'capitulated' (surrendered to the invading Nazi forces) in May, 1940.*

things. But somehow we children still managed to have fun. Yesterday Father told me we were going into hiding. Where, he wouldn't say. At five o'clock this morning Mother woke me and told me to hurry and get dressed. I was to put on as many clothes as I could. It would look too suspicious if we walked along carrying suitcases. It wasn't until we were on our way that I learned where we were going. Our hiding place was to be upstairs in the building where Father used to have his business. Three other people were coming in with us . . . the Van Daans and their son   70
Peter . . . Father knew the Van Daans but we had never met them . . .

(During the last lines the curtain rises on the scene. The lights dim on. ANNE'S VOICE fades out.)

yellow stars *By 1941 the Nazis had decided to put in place the 'final solution' to the Jewish 'problem': the total extermination of all Jews. At first, Jews were forced to wear a yellow star (see the note on the Star of David: page 6) and their lives became a misery as restrictions were imposed upon what they could do. Later they were sent off to concentration camps where many were killed or died of starvation and disease.*

to turn in my bike *Jews had to give up their bicycles as one of the many restrictions on their movements.*

DISCUSSION: Read the extract from Anne's diary on pages 119 – 121 and discuss what you know about the Nazis and their persecution of the Jews.

DISCUSSION: This play starts and ends in November 1945 while all the scenes in between the first and last take place earlier – between July 1942 and July 1944. Discuss as a class othet stories – films, television drama – that work in the same way. What are the advantages of this method of telling a story.

ACT 1 ❖ SCENE 2

It is early morning, July, 1942. The rooms are bare, as before, but they are now clean and orderly.

MR VAN DAAN, a tall portly man in his late forties, is in the main room, pacing up and down, nervously smoking a cigarette. His clothes and overcoat are expensive and well cut.

MRS VAN DAAN sits on the couch, clutching her possessions, a hatbox, bags, etc. She is a pretty woman in her early forties. She wears a fur coat over her other clothes.

PETER VAN DAAN is standing at the window of the room on the right, looking down at the street below. He is a shy, awkward boy of sixteen. He wears a cap, a raincoat, and long Dutch trousers, like 'plus fours'. At his feet is a black case, a carrier for his cat.

The yellow Star of David is conspicuous on all of their clothes.

MRS VAN DAAN	*(Rising, nervous, excited.)* Something's happened to them! I know it!	1
MR VAN DAAN	Now, Kerli!	
MRS VAN DAAN	Mr Frank said they'd be here at seven o'clock. He said . . .	
MR VAN DAAN	They have two miles to walk. You can't expect . . .	
MRS VAN DAAN	They've been picked up. That's what's happened. They've been taken. . . .	

(MR VAN DAAN indicates that he hears someone coming.)

'**plus fours**' *Trousers that come to just below the knees (these days mainly worn by golfers.)*

Star of David *The Jewish emblem, used on the shield of King David, the second King of Israel. This is the star that Jews were forced to wear on their clothing.*

MR VAN DAAN	You see?

(PETER takes up his carrier and his schoolbag, etc., and goes into the main room as MR FRANK comes up the stair-well from below. MR FRANK looks much younger now. His movements are brisk, his manner confident. He wears an overcoat and carries his hat and a small cardboard box. He crosses to the VAN DAANS, shaking hands with each of them.)   10

MR FRANK   Mrs Van Daan, Mr Van Daan, Peter. *(Then, in explanation of their lateness.)* There were too many of the Green Police on the streets . . . we had to take the long way around.

(Up the steps come MARGOT FRANK, MRS FRANK, MIEP – not pregnant now – and MR KRALER. All of them carry bags, packages, and so forth. The Star of David is conspicuous on all of the FRANKS' clothing. MARGOT is eighteen, beautiful, quiet, shy. MRS FRANK is a young mother, gently bred, reserved. She, like MR FRANK, has a slight German accent. MR KRALER is a Dutchman, dependable, kindly.   20

As MR KRALER and MIEP go upstage to put down their parcels, Mrs Frank turns back to call ANNE.)

MRS FRANK   Anne?

(ANNE comes running up the stairs. She is thirteen, quick in her movements, interested in everything, mercurial in her emotions. She wears a cape, long wool socks and carries a schoolbag.)   30

MR FRANK   *(Introducing them.)* My wife, Edith. Mr and Mrs Van Daan *(MRS FRANK hurries over, shaking hands with them.)* . . . their son, Peter . . . my daughters, Margot and Anne.

Green Police *The ordinary state police (as distinct from the Gestapo, whose purpose was to control 'political crimes'.) The Dutch called them Green Police because of the colour of their uniforms.*

mercurial in her emotions *She changes her feelings very quickly and unpredictably.*

	(*Anne gives a polite little curtsey as she shakes MR VAN DAAN'S hand. Then she immediately starts off on a tour of investigation of her hew home, going upstairs to the attic room.*	
	MIEP and MR KRALER are putting the various things they have brought on the shelves.)	
MR KRALER	I'm sorry there is still so much confusion.	40
MR FRANK	Please. Don't think of it. After all, we'll have plenty of leisure to arrange everything ourselves.	
MIEP	(*To MRS FRANK.*) We put the stores of food you sent in here. Your drugs are here . . . soap, linen here.	
MRS FRANK	Thank you , Miep.	
MIEP	I made up the beds . . . the way Mr Frank and Mr Kraler said. (*She starts out.*) Forgive me. I have to hurry. I've got to go to the other side of town to get some ration books for you.	
MRS VAN DAAN	Ration books? If they see our names on ration books, they'll know we're here.	50
MR KRALER	There isn't anything . . .	
MIEP	Don't worry. Your names won't be on them. (*As she hurries out.*) I'll be up later.	
MR FRANK	Thank you, Miep.	
MRS FRANK	(*To MR KRALER.*) It's illegal, then, the ration books? We've never done anything illegal.	

MR KRALER and MIEP — } *Together*

drugs *'medicines'*

ration books *During the war, food and many other everyday necessities were in short supply. Each person was allowed only a small quantity of meat, for example, and the butcher would stamp their ration book to show that they had received it.*

MR FRANK	We won't be living here exactly according to regulations.
	(As MR KRALER reassures MRS FRANK, he takes various small things, such as matches, soap, etc., from his pockets, handing them to her.) 60
MR KRALER	This isn't the black market, Mrs Frank. This is what we call the white market . . . helping all of the hundreds and hundreds who are hiding out in Amsterdam.
	(The carillon is heard playing the quarter-hour before eight. MR KRALER looks at this watch. ANNE stops at the window as she comes down the stairs.)
ANNE	It's the Westertoren!
MR KRALER	I must go. I must be out of here and downstairs in the office before the workmen get here. *(He starts for the stairs leading* 70 *out.)* Miep or I, or both of us, will be up each day to bring you food and news and find out what your needs are. Tomorrow I'll get you a better bolt for the door at the foot of the stairs. It needs a bolt that you can throw yourself and open only at our signal. *(To MR FRANK.)* Oh . . . You'll tell them about the noise?
MR FRANK	I'll tell them.
MR KRALER	Goodbye then for the moment. I'll come up again, after the workmen leave.
MR FRANK	Goodbye, Mr Kraler. 80
MRS FRANK	*(Shaking his hand.)* How can we thank you?
	(The others murmur their goodbyes.)

. . . according to regulations *Living in hiding, the Franks are breaking the rules imposed by the Nazis.*

black market *Some people managed to get hold of goods that were rationed and sell them illegally on the 'black market'. As Mr Kraler's dealings are for a good cause, he calls it the 'white market'.*

MR KRALER	I never thought I'd live to see the day when a man like Mr Frank would have to go into hiding. When you think –

(He breaks off, going out. MR FRANK follows him down the steps, bolting the door after him. In the interval before he returns, PETER goes over to MARGOT, shaking hands with her. As MR FRANK comes back up the steps, MRS FRANK questions him anxiously.)

MRS FRANK	What did he mean, 'about the noise'?	90
MR FRANK	First let us take off some of these clothes.	

(They all start to take off garment after garment. On each of their coats, sweaters, blouses, suits, dresses, is another yellow Star of David. MR and MRS FRANK are undressed quite simply. The others wear several things, sweaters, extra dresses, bathrobes, aprons, nightgowns, etc.)

MR VAN DAAN	It's a wonder we weren't arrested, walking along the streets . . . Petronella with a fur coat in July . . . and that cat of Peter's crying all the way.	
ANNE	*(As she is removing a pair of panties.)* A cat?	100
MRS FRANK	*(Shocked.)* Anne, please!	
ANNE	It's all right. I've got on three more.	

(She pulls off two more. Finally, as they have all removed their surplus clothes, they look to MR FRANK, waiting for him to speak.)

MR FRANK	Now. About the noise. While the men are in the building below, we must have complete quiet. Every sound can be heard down there, not only in the workrooms, but in the offices too. The men come at about eight-thirty, and leave at about five-thirty. So, to be perfectly safe, from eight in the morning until six in the evening we must move only when it is necessary, and then in stocking-feet. We must not speak above a whisper. We must not run any water. We cannot use the sink, or even, forgive me, the W.C. The	110

pipes go down through the workrooms. It would be heard. No rubbish . . . *(MR FRANK stops abruptly as he hears the sound of marching feet from the street below. Everyone is motionless, paralysed with fear. MR FRANK goes quietly into the room on the right to look down out of the window. ANNE runs after him, peering out with him. The tramping feet pass without stopping. The tension is relieved. MR FRANK, followed by ANNE, returns to the main room and resumes his instructions to the group.)* . . . No rubbish, must ever be thrown out which might reveal that someone is living up here . . . not even a potato peeling. We must burn everything in the stove at night. This is the way we must live until it is over, if we are to survive.   120

(There is silence for a second.)

MRS FRANK   Until it is over.

MR FRANK   *(Reassuringly.)* After six we can move about . . . we can talk   130
and laugh and have our supper and read and play games . . . just as we would at home. *(He looks at his watch.)* And now I think it would be wise if we all went to our rooms, and were settled before eight o'clock. Mrs Van Daan, you and your husband will be upstairs. I regret that there's no place up there for Peter. But he will be here, near us. This will be our common room, where we'll meet to talk and eat and read, like one family.

MR VAN DAAN   And where do you and Mrs Frank sleep?

MR FRANK   This room is also our bedroom.   140

MRS VAN DAAN   That isn't right. We'll sleep here and you take the room upstairs.

MR VAN DAAN   It's your place.

⎫
⎬ *Together*
⎭

MR FRANK   Please, I've thought this out for weeks. It's the best arrangement. The only arrangement.

MRS VAN DAAN   *(To MR FRANK.)* Never, never can we thank you. *(Then to*

MRS FRANK.) I don't know what would have happened to us, if it hadn't been for Mr Frank.

MR FRANK   You don't know how your husband helped me when I came to this country . . . knowing no one . . . not able to speak the language. I can never repay him for that. *(Going to VAN DAAN.)* May I help you with your things?   150

MR VAN DAAN   No, no. *(To MRS VAN DAAN.)* Come along, liefje.

MRS VAN DAAN   You'll be all right, Peter? You're not afraid?

PETER   *(Embarrassed.)* Please, Mother.

(They start up the stairs to the attic room above. MR FRANK turns to MRS FRANK.)

MR FRANK   You too must have some rest, Edith. You didn't close your eyes last night. Nor you, Margot.

ANNE   I slept, Father. Wasn't that funny? I knew it was the last night in my own bed, and yet I slept soundly.   160

MR FRANK   I'm glad Anne. Now you'll be able to help me straighten things in here. *(To MRS FRANK and MARGOT.)* Come with me . . . You and Margot rest in this room for the time being.

(He picks up their clothes, starting for the room on the right.)

MRS FRANK   You're sure . . .? I could help . . . And Anne hasn't had her milk . . .

MR FRANK   I'll give it to her. *(To ANNE and PETER.)* Anne, Peter . . . it's best that you take off your shoes now, before you forget.

(He leads the way to the room, followed by MARGOT.)   170

MRS FRANK   You're sure you're not tired, Anne?

---

liefje 'darling' Pronounced **leaf-yer**.

ANNE	I feel fine, I'm going to help Father.
MRS FRANK	Peter, I'm glad you are to be with us.
PETER	Yes, Mrs Frank.
	(MRS FRANK goes to join MR FRANK and MARGOT.
	During the following scene MR FRANK helps MARGOT and MRS FRANK to hang up their clothes. Then he persuades them both to lie down and rest. The VAN DAANS in their room above settle themselves. In the main room ANNE and PETER remove their shoes. PETER takes his cat out of the carrier.) 180
ANNE	What's your cat's name?
PETER	Mouschi.
ANNE	Mouschi! Mouschi! Mouschi! *(She picks up the cat, walking away with it. To PETER.)* I love cats. I have one . . . a darling little cat. But they made me leave her behind. I left some food and a note for the neighbours to take care of her . . . I'm going to miss her terribly. What is yours? A him or a her?
PETER	He's a tom. He doesn't like strangers.
	(He takes the cat from her, putting it back in its carrier.) 190
ANNE	*(Unabashed.)* Then I'll have to stop being a stranger won't I? Is he fixed?
PETER	*(Startled.)* Huh?
ANNE	Did you have him fixed?
PETER	No.
ANNE	Oh, you ought to have him fixed – to keep him from – you

 fixed *'neutered' (castrated, so that he cannot make other cats pregnant.)*

	know, fighting. Where did you go to school?
PETER	Jewish Secondary.
ANNE	But that's where Margot and I go! I never saw you around.
PETER	I used to see you . . . sometimes . . . **200**
ANNE	You did?
PETER	. . . in the school yard. You were always in the middle of a bunch of kids.
	(He takes a penknife from his pocket.)
ANNE	Why didn't you ever come over?
PETER	I'm sort of a lone wolf.
	(He starts to rip off his Star of David.)
ANNE	What are you doing?
PETER	Taking if off.
ANNE	But you can't do that. They'll arrest you if you go out **210** without your star.
	(He tosses his knife on the table.)
PETER	Who's going out?
ANNE	Why, of course! You're right! Of course we don't need them any more. *(She picks up his knife and starts to take her star off.)* I wonder what our friends will think when we don't show up today?
PETER	I didn't have any dates with anyone.
ANNE	Oh, I did. I have a date with Jopie to go and play ping-pong at her house. Do you know Jopie de Waal? **220**
PETER	No.
ANNE	Jopie's my best friend. I wonder what she'll think when she telephones and there's no answer? . . . Probably she'll go

over to the house . . . I wonder what she'll think . . . we left everything as if we'd suddenly been called away . . . breakfast dishes in the sink . . . beds not made . . . *(As she pulls off her star the cloth underneath shows clearly the colour and form of the star.)* Look! It's still there! *(PETER goes over to the stove with his star.)* What're you going to do with yours?

PETER	Burn it.	230

ANNE *(She starts to throw hers in, and cannot.)* It's funny, I can't throw mine away. I don't know why.

PETER You can't throw . . .? Something they branded you with . . .? That they made you wear so they could spit on you?

ANNE I know. I know. But after all, it is the Star of David, isn't it?

(In the bedroom, right, MARGOT and MRS FRANK are lying down. MR FRANK starts quietly out.)

PETER Maybe it's different for a girl.

(MR FRANK comes into the main room.) 240

MR FRANK Forgive me, Peter. Now let me see. We must find a bed for your cat. *(He goes to a cupboard.)* I'm glad you brought your cat. Anne was feeling so badly about hers. *(Getting a small worn wash-tub.)* Here we are. Will it be comfortable in that?

PETER *(Gathering his things.)* Thanks.

MR FRANK *(Opening the door of the room on the left.)* And here is your room. But I warn you, Peter, you can't grow any more. Not an inch, or you'll have to sleep with your feet out of the skylight. Are you hungry?

PETER	No.	250

MR FRANK We have some bread and butter.

PETER No, thank you.

MR FRANK You can have it for luncheon then. And tonight we will have a real supper . . . our first supper together.

PETER Thanks. Thanks.

(He goes into his room. During the following scene he arranges his possessions in his new room.)

MR FRANK That's a nice boy, Peter.

ANNE He's awfully shy, isn't he?

MR FRANK You'll like him, I know.   260

ANNE I certainly hope so, since he's the only boy I'm likely to see for months and months.

(MR FRANK sits down, taking off his shoes.)

MR FRANK Annele, there's a box there. Will you open it?

(He indicates a carton on the couch. ANNE brings it to the centre table. In the street below there is the sound of children playing.)

ANNE *(As she opens the carton.)* You know the way I'm going to think of it here? I'm going to think of it as a boarding house. A very peculiar summer boarding house, like the one that we – *(She breaks off as she pulls out some photographs.)*   270 Father! My film stars! I was wondering where they were! I was looking for them this morning . . . and Queen Wilhelmina! How wonderful!

MR FRANK There's something more. Go on. Look further.

(He goes over to the sink, pouring a glass of milk from a thermos bottle.)

ANNE *(Pulling out a pasteboard-bound book.)* A diary! *(She throws her arms around here father.)* I've never had a diary. And I've always longed for one. *(She looks around the room.)* Pencil,

---

boarding house *A house in which people go to stay on holiday.*

Queen Wilhelmina *Anne has a picture of the Dutch Queen.*

pencil, pencil, pencil. *(She starts down the stairs.)* I'm going down to the office to get a pencil. **280**

MR FRANK   Anne! No!

(He goes after her, catching her by the arm and pulling her back.)

ANNE   *(Startled.)* But there's no one in the building now.

MR FRANK   It doesn't matter. I don't want you ever to go beyond that door.

ANNE   *(Sobered.)* Never . . .? Not even at night-time, when everyone is gone? Or on Sundays? Can't I go down to listen to the radio?

MR FRANK   Never. I am sorry, Anneke. It isn't safe. No, you must never go beyond that door. **290**

(For the first time ANNE realises what 'going into hiding' means.)

ANNE   I see.

MR FRANK   It'll be hard, I know. But always remember this, Anneke. There are no walls, there are no bolts, no locks that anyone can put on your mind. Miep will bring us books. We will read history, poetry, mythology. *(He gives her the glass of milk.)* Here's your milk. *(With his arm about her, they go over to the couch, sitting down side by side.)* As a matter of fact, between us, Anne, being here has certain advantages for **300** you. For instance, you remember the battle you had with your mother the other day on the subject of overshoes? You said you'd rather die than wear overshoes? But in the end you had to wear them? Well now, you see, for as long as we are here you will never have to wear overshoes! Isn't that

overshoes *Overshoes were worn outside a person's normal shoes to keep them dry in bad weather.*

good? And the coat that you inherited from Margot, you won't have to wear that any more. And the piano! You won't have to practise on the piano. I tell you this is going to be a fine life for you!

(ANNE'S panic is gone. PETER appears in the doorway of his room with a saucer in his hand. He is carrying his cat.) 310

PETER   I . . . I . . . I thought I'd better get some water for Mouschi before . . .

MR FRANK   Of course.

(As he starts towards the sink the carillon begins to chime the hour of eight. He tiptoes to the window at the back and looks down at the street below. He turns to PETER, indicating in pantomime that it is too late. PETER starts back for his room. He steps on a creaking board. The three of them are frozen for a minute in fear. As PETER starts away again, ANNE tiptoes over 320 *to him and pours some of the milk from her glass into the saucer for the cat. PETER squats on the floor, putting the milk before the cat. MR FRANK gives ANNE his fountain pen, and then goes into the room on the right. For a second ANNE watches the cat, then she goes over to the centre table, and opens her diary.*

In the room on the right, MRS FRANK has sat up quickly at the sound of the carillon. MR FRANK comes in and sits down beside her on the couch, his arm comfortingly around her.

Upstairs, in the attic room, MR and MRS VAN DAAN have hung their clothes in the cupboard and are now seated on the iron bed. 330 *MRS VAN DAAN leans back exhausted. MR VAN DAAN fans her with a newspaper.*

ANNE starts to write in her diary. The lights dim out, the curtain falls. In the darkness ANNE'S VOICE comes to us again, faintly at first, and then with growing strength.)

ANNE'S VOICE.   I expect I should be describing what it feels like to go into hiding. But I really don't know yet myself. I only know it's funny never to be able to go outdoors . . . never to breathe

fresh air . . . never to run and shout and jump. It's the
silence in the nights that frightens me most. Every time I   340
hear a creak in the house, or a step on the street outside,
I'm sure they're coming for us. The days aren't so bad. At
least we know that Miep and Mr Kraler are down there
below us in the office. Our protectors, we call them. I asked
Father what would happen to them if the Nazis found out
they were hiding us. Pim said that they would suffer the
same fate that we would . . . Imagine! They know this, and
yet when they come up here, they're always cheerful and
gay as if there were nothing in the world to bother
them . . . Friday, the twenty-first of August, nineteen forty-   350
two. Today I'm going to tell you our general news. Mother
is unbearable. She insists on treating me like a baby, which I
loathe. Otherwise things are going better. The weather
is . . .

(As ANNE'S VOICE is fading out, the curtain rises on the scene.)

WRITING: Draw up the poster which might have been pinned to the attic wall, listing the 'Rules of the House' based upon what Mr Frank says. Discuss which other rules you think might be sensible.

HOT-SEATING: In groups of four, one person takes on the character of Anne while the others question her on how she feels about coming to live in the attic. (Notice how different Anne's behaviour and reactions are to other people's.)

DISCUSSION: As a class, discuss the things you already know about Peter. What kind of person is he? How is he likely to get on, living in the attic for a long time? Refer to details in the text, using quotations, to support what you say.

DISCUSSION: As a class, discuss the many practical difficulties that might arise when two families are living together in this way.

ARTWORK: Discuss in pairs where everybody sleeps and eats in the attic, and then draw a diagram or picture to make it clear. (Keep your diagram.)

WRITING: Imagine that you are producing an 'underground' newspaper for the Dutch Resistance (the people fighting secretly against the Nazis.) Write an article in which you offer practical advice to anybody who might be thinking of sheltering people.

WRITING: Start building up 'dossiers' on three of the characters who interest you most. First give some factual details (name, approximate age, relationship to other characters, profession, etc); then begin to make notes on their personalities and characters based on things that they have said or done, or things that others have said about them.

WRITING: List details that you think are significant in view of what is going to happen in the story, e.g. who is Miep Gies, and what does Mr Frank say that provides a clue about what she has doen for the family?

ARTWORK: In pairs, check that you know the names of all the characters so far: note their ages and how they are related to each other. Use diagrams like this:

Mr Smith (late 40s)	=	Mrs Smith (early 40s)

Jack (16)		Jill (12)

DISCUSSION: From your knowledge of World war II (and *Dad's Army*!) discuss what ration books were for and why they were important. What was the black market?

ACT 1 ❖ SCENE 3

It is a little after six o'clock in the evening, two months later.

> *MARGOT is in the bedroom at the right, studying. MR VAN DAAN is lying down in the attic room above.*

> *The rest of the 'family' is in the main room. ANNE and PETER sit opposite each other at the centre table, where they have been doing their lessons. MRS FRANK is on the couch. MRS VAN DAAN is seated with her fur coat, on which she has been sewing, in her lap. None of them are wearing their shoes.*

> *Their eyes are on MR FRANK, waiting for him to give them the signal which will release them from their day-long quiet. MR FRANK, his shoes in his hand, stands looking down out of the window at the back, watching to be sure that all of the workmen have left the building below.*

> *After a few seconds of motionless silence, MR FRANK turns from the window.*

MR FRANK	*(Quietly, to the group.)* It's safe now. The last workman has left.	1
	(There is an immediate stir of relief.)	
ANNE	*(Her pent-up energy exploding.)* WHEE!	
MRS FRANK	*(Startled, amused.)* Anne!	
MRS VAN DAAN	I'm first for the W.C.	
	(She hurries off to the bathroom. MRS FRANK puts on her shoes and starts up to the sink to prepare supper. ANNE sneaks PETER'S shoes from under the table and hides them behind her back. MR FRANK goes into MARGOT'S room.)	10
MR FRANK	*(To Margot.)* Six o'clock. School's over.	
	(MARGOT gets up, stretching. MR FRANK sits down to put on his shoes. In the main room PETER tries to find his.)	
PETER	*(To Anne.)* Have you seen my shoes?	

ANNE	*(Innocently.)* Your shoes?
PETER	You've taken them, haven't you?
ANNE	I don't know what you're talking about.
PETER	You're going to be sorry!
ANNE	Am !?
	(PETER goes after her. ANNE, with his shoes in her hand, runs 20 from him, dodging behind her mother.)
MRS FRANK	*(Protesting.)* Anne, dear!
PETER	Wait till I get you!
ANNE	I'm waiting! *(PETER makes a lunge for her. They both fall to the floor. PETER pins her down, wrestling with her to get the shoes.)* Don't! Don't! Peter, stop it. Ouch!
MRS FRANK	Anne! . . . Peter!
	(Suddenly PETER becomes self-conscious. He grabs his shoes roughly and starts for his room.)
ANNE	*(Following him.)* Peter, where are you going? Come dance 30 with me.
PETER	I tell you I don't know how.
ANNE	I'll teach you.
PETER	I'm going to give Mouschi his dinner.
ANNE	Can I watch?
PETER	He doesn't like people around while he eats.
ANNE	Peter, please.
PETER	No!
	(He goes into his room. ANNE slams his door after him.)
MRS FRANK	Anne, dear, I think you shouldn't play like that with Peter. 40 It's not dignified.

ANNE	Who cares if it's dignified? I don't want to be dignified.
	(MR FRANK and MARGOT come from the room on the right. MARGOT goes to help her mother. MR FRANK starts for the centre table to correct MARGOT'S school papers.)
MRS FRANK	*(To ANNE.)* You complain that I don't treat you like a grown-up. But when I do, you resent it.
ANNE	I only want some fun . . . someone to laugh and clown with . . . After you've sat still all day and hardly moved, you've got to have some fun. I don't know what's the matter with that boy. 50
MR FRANK	He isn't used to girls. Give him a little time.
ANNE	Time? Isn't two months time? I could cry. *(Catching hold of MARGOT.)* Come on, Margot . . . dance with me. Come on, please.
MARGOT	I have to help with supper.
ANNE	You know we're going to forget how to dance . . . When we get out we won't remember a thing.
	(She starts to sing and dance by herself. MR FRANK takes her in his arms, waltzing with her. MRS VAN DAAN comes in from the bedroom.) 60
MRS VAN DAAN	Next? *(She looks around as she starts putting on her shoes.)* Where's Peter?
ANNE	*(As they are dancing.)* Where would he be!
MRS VAN DAAN	He hasn't finished his lessons, has he? His father'll kill him if he catches him in there with that cat and his work not done. *(MR FRANK and ANNE finish their dance. They bow to each other with extravagant formality.)* Anne, get him out of there, will you?
ANNE	*(At PETER'S door.)* Peter? Peter? 70
PETER	*(Opening the door a crack.)* What is it?

ANNE	Your mother says to come out.
PETER	I'm giving Mouschi his dinner.
MRS VAN DAAN	You know what your father says.
	(She sits on the couch, sewing on the lining of her fur coat.)
PETER	For heaven's sake. I haven't even looked at him since lunch.
MRS VAN DAAN	I'm just telling you, that's all.
ANNE	I'll feed him.
PETER	I don't want you in there.
MRS VAN DAAN	Peter!
PETER	*(To ANNE.)* Then give him his dinner and come right out, you hear?
	(He comes back to the table, ANNE shuts the door of PETER'S room after her and disappears behind the curtain covering his closet.)
MRS VAN DAAN	*(To PETER.)* Now is that any way to talk to your little girl friend?
PETER	Mother . . . for heaven's sake . . . will you please stop saying that?
MRS VAN DAAN	Look at him blush! Look at him!
PETER	Please! I'm not . . . anyway . . . let me alone, will you?
MRS VAN DAAN	He acts like it was something to be ashamed of. It's nothing to be ashamed of, to have a little girl friend.
PETER	You're crazy. She's only thirteen.
MRS VAN DAAN	So what? And you're sixteen. Just perfect. Your father's ten years older than I am. *(To MR FRANK.)* I warn you, Mr Frank, if this war lasts much longer, we're going to be related and then . . .
MR FRANK	Mazeltov!

80

90

24

MRS FRANK	*(Deliberately changing the conversation.)* I wonder where Miep 100 is. She's usually so prompt.
	(Suddenly everything else is forgotten as they hear the sound of an automobile coming to a screeching stop in the street below. They are tense, motionless in their terror. The car starts away. A wave of relief sweeps over them. They pick up their occupations again. ANNE flings open the door of PETER'S room, making a dramatic entrance. She is dressed in PETER'S clothes. PETER looks at her in fury. The others are amused.)
ANNE	Good evening, everyone. Forgive me if I don't stay. *(She jumps up on a chair.)* I have a friend waiting for me in there. 110 My friend Tom. Tom Cat. Some people say that we look alike. But Tom, has the most beautiful whiskers, and I have only a little fuzz. I am hoping . . . in time . . .
PETER	All right, Mrs Quack-Quack!
ANNE	*(Outraged – jumping down.)* Peter!
PETER	I heard about you . . . How you talked so much in class they called you Mrs Quack Quack. How Mr Smitter made you write a composition . . . ' "Quack, quack", said Mrs Quack Quack.'
ANNE	Well, go on. Tell them the rest. How it was so good he read 120 it out loud to the class and then read it to all his other classes!
PETER	Quack! Quack! Quack! . . . Quack . . . Quack . . .
	(ANNE pulls off the coat and trousers.)
ANNE	You are the most intolerable, insufferable boy I've ever met!

Mazeltov! *The Hebrew expression for 'Congratulations!'. It literally means 'Good luck!'.*

25

(She throws the clothes down the stair-well. PETER goes down after them.)

PETER Quack, quack, quack!

MRS VAN DAAN *(To ANNE.)* That's right, Anneke! Give it to him!

ANNE With all the boys in the world . . . Why I had to get locked up with one like you! . . .

PETER Quack, quack, quack, and from now on stay out of my room!

(As PETER passes her, ANNE put out her foot, tripping him. He picks himself up, and goes on into his room.)

MRS FRANK *(Quietly.)* Anne, dear . . . your hair. *(She feels ANNE'S forehead.)* You're warm. Are you feeling all right?

ANNE Please, Mother.

(She goes over to the centre table, slipping into her shoes.)

MRS FRANK *(Following her.)* You haven't a fever, have you?

ANNE *(Pulling away.)* No. No.

MRS FRANK You know we can't call a doctor here, ever. There's only one thing to do . . . watch carefully. Prevent an illness before it comes. Let me see your tongue.

ANNE Mother, this is perfectly absurd.

MRS FRANK Anne, dear, don't be such a baby. Let me see your tongue. *(As ANNE refuses, MRS FRANK appeals to MR FRANK.)* Otto . . . ?

MR FRANK You hear your mother, Anne.

(ANNE flicks out her tongue for a second, then turns away.)

MRS FRANK Come on – open up! *(As ANNE opens her mouth very wide.)* You seem all right . . . but perhaps an aspirin . . .

MRS VAN DAAN For heaven's sake, don't give that child any pills. I waited

130

140

150

for fifteen minutes this morning for her to come out of the W.C.

ANNE	I was washing my hair!
MR FRANK	I think there's nothing the matter with our Anne that a ride on her bike, or a visit with her friend Jopie de Waal wouldn't cure. Isn't that so, Anne?

(MR VAN DAAN comes down into the room. From outside we   160
hear faint sounds of bombers going over and a burst of
'ack-ack'.)

MR VAN DAAN	Miep not come yet?
MRS VAN DAAN	The workmen just left, a little while ago.
MR VAN DAAN	What's for dinner tonight?
MRS VAN DAAN	Beans.
MR VAN DAAN	Not again!
MRS VAN DAAN	Poor Putti! I know. But what can we do? That's all that Miep brought us.

(MR VAN DAAN starts to pace, his hands behind his back.   170
ANNE follows behind him, imitating him.)

ANNE	We are now in what is known as the 'bean cycle'. Beans boiled, beans *en casserole*, beans with strings, beans without strings . . .

(PETER has come out of his room. He slides into his place at the
table, becoming immediately absorbed in his studies.)

MR VAN DAAN	*(To PETER.)* I saw you . . . in there, playing with your cat.
MRS VAN DAAN	He just went in for a second, putting his coat away. He's

ack-ack *Anti-aircraft fire.*

been out here all the time, doing his lessons.

MR FRANK   (*Looking up from the papers.*) Anne, you got an excellent in   180
your history paper today . . . and very good in Latin.

ANNE   (*Sitting beside him.*) How about algebra?

MR FRANK   I'll have to make a confession. Up until now I've managed
to stay ahead of you in algebra. Today you caught up with
me. We'll leave to it Margot to correct.

ANNE   Isn't algebra *vile*, Pim!

MR FRANK   Vile!

MARGOT   (*To MR FRANK.*) How did I do?

ANNE   (*Getting up.*) Excellent, excellent, excellent, excellent!

MR FRANK   (*To MARGOT.*) You should have used the subjunctive   190
here . . .

MARGOT   Should !? . . . I thought . . . look here . . . I didn't use it
here . . .

(*The two become absorbed in the papers.*)

ANNE   Mrs Van Daan, may I try on your coat?

MRS FRANK   No, Anne.

MRS VAN DAAN   (*Giving it to ANNE.*) It's all right . . . but careful with it.
(*ANNE puts it on and struts with it.*) My father gave me that
the year before he died. He always bought the best that
money could buy.   200

ANNE   Mrs Van Daan, did you have a lot of boy friends before you
were married?

subjunctive *A term in grammar describing a form of the verb.*

MRS FRANK	Anne, that's a personal question. It's not courteous to ask personal questions.
MRS VAN DAAN	Oh, I don't mind. *(To ANNE)* Our house was always swarming with boys. When I was a girl we had . . .
MR VAN DAAN	Oh, God. Not again!
MRS VAN DAAN	*(Good-humoured.)* Shut up! *(without a pause, to ANNE. MR VAN DAAN mimics MRS VAN DAAN, speaking the first few words in unison with her.)* One summer we had a big house in Hilversum. The boys came buzzing round like bees around a jam pot. And when I was sixteen! . . . We were wearing our skirts very short those days and I had good-looking legs. *(She pulls up her skirt, going to MR FRANK.)* I still have 'em. I may not be as pretty as I used to be, but I still have my legs. How about it, Mr Frank?
MR VAN DAAN	All right. All right. We see them.
MRS VAN DAAN	I'm not asking you. I'm asking Mr Frank.
PETER	Mother, for heaven's sake.
MRS VAN DAAN	Oh, I embarrass you, do I? Well, I just hope the girl you marry has as good. *(Then to ANNE.)* My father used to worry about me, with so many boys hanging round. He told me, if any of them gets fresh, you say to him . . . 'Remember, Mr So-and-So, remember I'm a lady'.
ANNE	'Remember, Mr So-and-So, remember I'm a lady.'
	(She gives MRS VAN DAAN her coat.)
MR VAN DAAN	Look at you, talking that way in front of her! Don't you know she puts it all down in that diary?
MRS VAN DAAN	So, if she does? I'm only telling the truth!
	(ANNE stretches out, putting her ear to the floor, listening to what is going on below. The sound of the bombers fades away.)
MRS FRANK	*(Setting the table.)* Would you mind, Peter, if I moved you

210

220

230

over to the couch?

ANNE   *(Listening.)* Miep must have the radio on.

(PETER picks up his papers, going over to the couch beside MRS VAN DAAN.)

MR VAN DAAN   *(Accusingly, to PETER.)* Haven't you finished yet?

PETER   No.

MR VAN DAAN   You ought to be ashamed of yourself.   240

PETER   All right. All right. I'm a dunce. I'm a hopeless case. Why do I go on?

MRS VAN DAAN   You're not hopeless. Don't talk that way. It's just that you haven't anyone to help you, like the girls have. *(To MR FRANK.)* Maybe you could help him, Mr Frank?

MR FRANK   I'm sure that his father . . . ?

MR VAN DAAN   Not me. I can't do anything with him. He won't listen to me. You go ahead . . . if you want.

MR FRANK   *(Going to PETER.)* What about it, Peter? Shall we make our school co-educational?   250

MRS VAN DAAN   *(Kissing MR FRANK.)* You're an angel, Mr Frank. An angel. I don't know why I didn't met you before I met that one there. Here, sit down, Mr Frank . . . *(She forces him down on the couch beside PETER.)* Now, Peter, you listen to Mr Frank.

MR FRANK   It might be better for us to go into Peter's room.

(PETER jumps up eagerly, leading the way.)

MRS VAN DAAN   That's right. You go in there, Peter. You listen to Mr Frank. Mr Frank is a highly educated man.

(As MR FRANK is about to follow PETER into his room MRS FRANK stops him and wipes the lipstick from his lips. Then she closes the door after them.)   260

ANNE   *(On the floor, listening.)* Shh! I can hear a man's voice talking.

MR VAN DAAN	*(To ANNE.)* Isn't it bad enough here without your sprawling all over the place?
	(ANNE sits up.)
MRS VAN DAAN	*(To MR VAN DAAN.)* If you didn't smoke so much, you wouldn't be so bad-tempered.
MR VAN DAAN	Am I smoking. Do you see me smoking?
MRS VAN DAAN	Don't tell me you've used up all those cigarettes.
MR VAN DAAN	One package. Miep only brought me one package.
MRS VAN DAAN	It's a filthy habit anyway. It's a good time to break yourself.
MR VAN DAAN	Oh, stop it, please.
MRS VAN DAAN	You're smoking up all our money. You know that, don't you?
MR VAN DAAN	Will you shut up? *(During this, MRS FRANK and MARGOT have studiously kept their eyes down. But ANNE, seated on the floor, has been following the discussion interestedly. MR VAN DAAN turns to see her staring up at him.)* And what are you staring at?
ANNE	I never heard grown-ups quarrel before! I thought only children quarrelled.
MR VAN DAAN	This isn't a quarrel! It's a discussion. And I never heard children so rude before.
ANNE	*(Rising, indignantly.)* I, rude!
MR VAN DAAN	Yes!
MRS FRANK	*(Quickly.)* Anne, will you get me my knitting? *(ANNE goes to get it.)* I must remember, when Miep comes to ask her to bring me some more wool.
MARGOT	*(Going to her room.)* I need some hairpins and some soap. I made a list.
	(She goes into her bedroom to get the list.)

270

280

290

MRS FRANK	*(To Anne.)* Have you some library books for Miep when she comes?
ANNE	It's a wonder that Miep has a life of her own, the way we make her run errands for us. Please, Miep, get me some starch. Please take my hair out and have it cut. Tell me all the latest news, Miep. *(She goes over, kneeling on the couch beside MRS VAN DAAN.)* Did you know she was engaged? His name is Dirk, and Miep's afraid the Nazis will ship him off to Germany to work in one of their war plants. That's what they're doing with some of the young Dutchmen . . . they pick them up off the streets –
MR VAN DAAN	*(Interrupting.)* Don't you ever get tired of talking? Suppose you try keeping still for five minutes. Just five minutes.
	(He starts to pace again. Again ANNE follows him, mimicking him. MRS FRANK jumps up and takes her by the arm up to the sink, and gives her a glass of milk.)
MRS FRANK	Come here, Anne. It's time for your glass of milk.
MR VAN DAAN	Talk, talk, talk. I never heard such a child. Where is my . . . ? Every evening it's the same, talk, talk, talk. *(He looks around.)* Where's is my . . . ?
MRS VAN DAAN	What're you looking for?
MR VAN DAAN	My pipe. Have you seen my pipe?
MRS VAN DAAN	What good's a pipe? You haven't got any tobacco.
MR VAN DAAN	At least I'll have something to hold in my mouth! *(Opening MARGOT'S bedroom door.)* Margot, have you seen my pipe?
MARGOT	It was on the table last night.
	(ANNE puts her glass of milk on the table and picks up his pipe, hiding it behind her back.)
MR VAN DAAN	I know, I know. Anne, did you see my pipe? . . . Anne!
MRS FRANK	Anne, Mr Van Daan is speaking to you.

300

310

320

ANNE	Am I allowed to talk now?
MR VAN DAAN	You're the most aggravating . . . The trouble with you is, you've been spoiled. What you need is a good old-fashioned spanking.
ANNE	*(Mimicking MRS VAN DAAN.)* 'Remember, Mr So-and-So, remember I'm a lady.'
	(She thrusts the pipe into his mouth, then picks up her glass of milk. MARGOT comes out of the bedroom and places the list on the table.) 330
MR VAN DAAN	*(Restraining himself with difficulty.)* Why aren't you nice and quiet like your sister Margot? Why do you have to show off all the time? Let me give you a little advice, young lady. Men don't like that kind of thing in a girl. You know that? A man likes a girl who'll listen to him once in a while . . . a domestic girl, who'll keep her house shining for her husband . . . who loves to cook and sew and . . .
ANNE	I'd cut my throat first! I'd open my veins! I'm going to be remarkable! I'm going to Paris . . .
MR VAN DAAN	*(Scofffingly.)* Paris! 340
ANNE	. . . to study music and art.
MR VAN DAAN	Yeah! Yeah!
ANNE	I'm going to be a famous dancer or singer . . . or something wonderful.
	(She makes a wide gesture, spilling the glass of milk on the fur coat in MRS VAN DAAN'S lap. MARGOT rushes quickly over with a towel. ANNE tries to brush the milk off with her skirt.)
MRS VAN DAAN	Now look what you've done . . . you clumsy little fool! My beautiful fur coat my father gave me . . .
ANNE	I'm so sorry. 350
MRS VAN DAAN	What do you care! It isn't yours . . . So go on, ruin it. Do

	you know what that coat cost? Do you? And now look at it. Look at it!
ANNE	I'm very, very sorry.
MRS VAN DAAN	I could kill you for this. I could just kill you!
	(*MRS VAN DAAN goes up the stairs, clutching the coat. MR VAN DAAN starts after her.*)
MR VAN DAAN	Petronella . . . liefje! Liefje! . . . Come back . . . the supper . . . come back!
MRS FRANK	Anne, you must not behave in that way.
ANNE	It was an accident. Anyone can have an accident.
MRS FRANK	I don't mean that. I mean the answering back. You must not answer back. They are our guests. We must always show the greatest courtesy to them. We're all living under terrible tension. (*She stops as MARGOT indicates that MR VAN DAAN can hear. When he is gone she continues.*) That's why we must control ourselves . . . You don't hear Margot getting into arguments with them, do you? Watch Margot. She's always courteous with them. Never familiar. She keeps her distance. And they respect her for it. Try to be like Margot.
ANNE	And have them walk all over me, the way they do her? No, thanks!
MRS FRANK	I'm not afraid that anyone is going to walk all over you, Anne. I'm afraid for other people, that you'll walk on them. I don't know what happens to you, Anne. You are wild, self-willed. If I had ever talked to my mother as you talk to me . . .
ANNE	Things have changed. People aren't like that any more. 'Yes, Mother.' 'No, Mother.' 'Anything you say, Mother.' I've got to fight things out for myself! Make something of myself!
MRS FRANK	It isn't necessary to fight to do it. Margot doesn't fight, and isn't she . . . ?

360

370

380

ANNE	*(Violently rebellious.)* Margot! Margot! Margot! That's all I hear from everyone . . . how wonderful Margot is . . . 'Why aren't you like Margot?'
MARGOT	*(Protesting.)* Oh come on, Anne, don't be so . . .
ANNE	*(Paying no attention.)* Everything she does is right, and everything I do is wrong! I'm the goat around here! . . . You're all against me! . . . And you worst of all!

(She rushes off into her room and throws herself down on the couch, stifling her sobs. MRS FRANK sighs and starts towards the stove.) 390

MRS FRANK	*(To MARGOT.)* Let's put the soup on the stove . . . if there's anyone who cares to eat. Margot, will you take the bread out? *(MARGOT gets the bread from the cupboard.)* I don't know how we can go on living this way . . . I can't say a word to Anne . . . She flies at me . . .
MARGOT	You know Anne. In half an hour she'll be out here, laughing and joking.
MRS FRANK	And . . . *(She makes a motion upwards, indicating the VAN DAANS.)* . . . I told your father it wouldn't work . . . but no . . . no . . . he had to ask them, he said . . . he owed it to him, he said. Well, he knows now that I was right! These quarrels! . . . This bickering!

400

MARGOT	*(With a warning look.)* Shush. Shush.

(The buzzer for the door sounds. MRS FRANK gasps, startled.)

MRS FRANK	Every time I hear that sound, my heart stops!
MARGOT	*(Starting for PETER'S door.)* It's Miep. *(She knocks at the door.)* Father?

I'm the goat around here . . . 'the scapegoat'; the person everybody picks on and blames.

(MR FRANK comes quickly from PETER'S room.) 41

MR FRANK Thank you, Margot. *(As he goes down the steps to open the outer door.)* Has everyone his list?

MARGOT I'll get my books. *(Giving her mother a list.)* Here's your list. *(MARGOT goes into her and ANNE'S bedroom on the right. ANNE sits up, hiding her tears, as Margot comes in.)* Miep's here.

(MARGOT picks up her books and goes back. ANNE hurries over to the mirror, smoothing her hair.)

MR VAN DAAN *(Coming down the stairs.)* Is it Miep?

MARGOT Yes, Father's gone down to let her in. 42

MR VAN DAAN At last I'll have some cigarettes!

MR FRANK *(To MR VAN DAAN.)* I can't tell you how unhappy I am about Mrs Van Daan's coat. Anne should never have touched it.

MR VAN DAAN She'll be all right.

MRS FRANK Is there anything I can do?

MR VAN DAAN Don't worry.

(He turns to meet MIEP. But it is not MIEP who comes up the steps. It is MR KRALER, followed by MR FRANK. Their faces are grave. ANNE comes from the bedroom. PETER comes from his room.) 43

MRS FRANK Mr Kraler!

MR VAN DAAN How are you, Mr Kraler?

MARGOT This is a surprise.

MRS FRANK When Mr Kraler comes, the sun begins to shine.

MR VAN DAAN Miep is coming?

MR KRALER Not tonight.

(KRALER goes to MARGOT and MRS FRANK and ANNE,
shaking hands with them.)

MRS FRANK	Wouldn't you like a cup of coffee? . . . Or, better still, will you have supper with us?	440

MR FRANK Mr Kraler has something to talk over with us. Something has happened, he says, which demands an immediate decision.

MRS FRANK (Fearful.) What is it?

(MR KRALER sits down on the couch. As he talks he takes bread, cabbages, milk, etc., from his briefcase, giving them to MARGOT and ANNE to put away.)

MR KRALER Usually, when I come up here, I try to bring you some bit of good news. What's the use of telling you the bad news 450 when there's nothing that you can do about it? But today something has happened . . . Dirk . . . Miep's Dirk, you know, came to me just now. He tells me that he has a Jewish friend living near him. A dentist. He says he's in trouble. He begged me, could I do anything for this man? Could I find him a hiding place? . . . So I've come to you . . . I know it's a terrible thing to ask of you, living as you are, but would you take him in with you?

MR FRANK Of course we will.

MR KRALER (Rising.) It'll be just for a night or two . . . until I find some 460 other place. This happened so suddenly that I didn't know where to turn.

MR FRANK Where is he?

MR KRALER Downstairs in the office.

MR FRANK Good. Bring him up.

MR KRALER His name is Dussel . . . Jan Dussel.

MR FRANK Dussel . . . I think I know him.

MR KRALER	I'll get him.
	(He goes quickly down the steps and out. MR FRANK suddenly becomes conscious of the others.) 47
MR FRANK	Forgive me. I spoke without consulting you. But I knew you'd feel as I do.
MR VAN DAAN	There's no reason for you to consult anyone. This is your place. You have a right to do exactly as you please. The only thing I feel . . . there's so little food as it is . . . and to take in another person . . .
	(PETER turns away, ashamed of his father.)
MR FRANK	We can stretch the food a little. It's only for a few days.
MR VAN DAAN	You want to make a bet?
MRS FRANK	I think it's fine to have him. But, Otto, where are you going 48 to put him? Where?
PETER	He can have my bed. I can sleep on the floor. I wouldn't mind.
MR FRANK	That's good of you Peter. But your room's too small . . . even for *you*.
ANNE	I have a much better idea. I'll come in here with you and Mother, and Margot can take Peter's room and Peter can go in our room with Mr Dussel.
MARGOT	That's right. We could do that.
MR FRANK	No, Margot. You mustn't sleep in that room . . . neither you 49 nor Anne. Mouschi has caught some rats in there. Peter's brave. He doesn't mind.
ANNE	Then how about *this*. I'll come in here with you and Mother, and Mr Dussel can have my bed.
MRS FRANK	No. No. *No!* Margot will come in here with us and he can have her bed. It's the only way. Margot bring your things in here. Help her, Anne.

(MARGOT hurries into her room to get her things.)

ANNE   *(To her mother.)* Why Margot? Why can't I come in here?

MRS FRANK   Because it wouldn't be proper for Margot to sleep with a . . .   500
Please, Anne. Don't argue, Please.

ANNE starts slowly away.

MR FRANK   *(To ANNE.)* You don't mind sharing your room with Mr
Dussel, to you Anne?

ANNE   No. No, of course not.

MR FRANK   Good. *(ANNE goes off into her bedroom, helping MARGOT. MR
FRANK starts to search in the cupboards.)* Where's the cognac?

MRS FRANK   It's there. But, Otto, I was saving it in case of illness.

MR FRANK   I think we couldn't find a better time to use it. Peter, will
you get five glasses for me?   510

*(PETER goes for the glasses. MARGOT comes out of her
bedroom, carrying her possessions, which she hangs behind a
curtain in the main room. MR FRANK finds the cognac and
pours it into the five glasses that PETER brings him. MR VAN
DAAN stands looking on sourly. MRS VAN DAAN comes
downstairs and looks around at all the bustle.)*

MRS VAN DAAN   What's happening? What's going on?

MR VAN DAAN   Someone's moving in with us.

MRS VAN DAAN   In here. You're joking?

MARGOT   It's only for a night or two . . . until Mr Kraler finds him   520
another place.

MR VAN DAAN   Yeah! Yeah!

cognac *Expensive French brandy (pronounced* con-yack.*)*

(*MR FRANK hurries over as MR KRALER and DUSSEL come up. DUSSEL is a man in his late fifties, meticulous, finicky . . . bewildered now. He wears a raincoat. He carries a briefcase, stuffed full, and a small medicine case.*)

MR FRANK   Come in, Mr Dussel.

MR KRALER   This is Mr Frank.

DUSSEL   Mr Otto Frank?

MR FRANK   Yes. Let me take your things. (*He takes the hat and briefcase,*   530
but DUSSEL clings to his medicine case.*) This is my wife
Edith . . . Mr and Mrs Van Daan . . . their son, Peter . . . and
my daughters, Margot and Anne.

(*DUSSEL shakes hands with everyone.*)

MR KRALER   Thank you, Mr Frank. Thank you all. Mr Dussel, I leave you
in good hands. Oh . . . Dirk's coat.

(*DUSSEL hurriedly takes off the raincoat, giving it to
MR KRALER. Underneath is his white dentist's jacket, with a
yellow Star of David on it.*)

DUSSEL   (*To MR KRALER.*) What can I say to thank you . . .?   540

MRS FRANK   (*To DUSSEL.*) Mr Kraler and Miep . . . They're our life line.
Without them we couldn't live.

MR KRALER   Please. Please. You make us seem very heroic. It isn't that at
all. We simply don't like the Nazis. (*To MR FRANK, who
offers him a drink.*) No, thanks. (*Then going on.*) We don't like
their methods. We don't like . . .

MR FRANK   (*Smiling.*) I know. I know. 'No ones going to tell us
Dutchmen what to do with our damn Jews!'

MR KRALER   (*To DUSSEL.*) Pay no attention to Mr Frank. I'll be up
tomorrow to see that they're treating you right. (*To*   550
MR FRANK.*) Don't trouble to come down again. Peter will
bolt the door after me, won't you, Peter?

PETER	Yes, sir.
MR FRANK	Thank you, Peter. I'll do it.
MR KRALER	Good night. Good night.
GROUP	Good night, Mr Kraler. We'll see you tomorrow . . .
	(MR KRALER goes out with MR FRANK. MRS FRANK gives each one of the 'grown-ups' a glass of cognac.)
MRS FRANK	Please, Mr Dussel, sit down.
	(MR DUSSEL, sinks into a chair. MRS FRANK gives him a glass of cognac.) 560
DUSSEL.	I'm dreaming. I know it. I can't believe my eyes. Mr Otto Frank here! *(To MRS FRANK)* You're not in Switzerland then? A woman told me . . . She said she'd gone to your house . . . the door was open, everything was in disorder, dishes in the sink. She said she found a piece of paper in the wastebasket with an address scribbled on it . . . an address in Zurich. She said you must have escaped to Zurich.
ANNE	Father put that there purposely . . . just so people would think that very thing! 570
DUSSEL	And you've been *here* all the time?
MRS FRANK	All the time . . . ever since July.
	(ANNE speaks to her father as he comes back.)
ANNE	It worked, Pim . . . the address you left! Mr Dussel says that people believe we escaped to Switzerland.
MR FRANK	I'm glad . . . And now let's have a little drink to welcome Mr Dussel. *(Before they can drink, MR DUSSEL bolts his drink. MR FRANK smiles and raises his glass.)* To Mr Dussel. Welcome. We're very honoured to have you with us.
MRS FRANK	To Mr Dussel, welcome. 580
	(The VAN DAAN'S murmur a welcome. The 'grown-ups' drink.)

41

MRS VAN DAAN	Um. That was good.
MR VAN DAAN	Did Mr Kraler warn you that you won't get much to eat here? You can imagine . . . three ration books among the seven of us . . . and now you make eight.
	(PETER walks away, humiliated. Outside a street organ is heard dimly.)
DUSSEL	*(Rising.)* Mr Van Daan, you don't realise what is happening outside that you should warn me of such a thing like that. You don't realise what's going on . . . *(As MR VAN DAAN* 590 *starts his characteristic pacing, DUSSEL turns to speak to the others.)* Right here in Amsterdam every day hundreds of Jews disappear . . . They surround a block and search house by house. Children come home from school to find their parents gone. Hundreds are being deported . . . people that you and I know . . . the Hallensteins . . . the Wessels . . .
MRS FRANK	*(In tears.)* Oh, no. No!
DUSSEL	They get their call-up notice . . . come to the Jewish theatre on such and such a day and hour . . . bring only what you can carry in a rucksack. And if you refuse the call-up notice, 600 then they come and drag you from home and ship you off to Mauthausen. The death camp!
MRS FRANK	We didn't know that things had got so much worse.
DUSSEL	Forgive me for speaking so.
ANNE	*(Coming to DUSSEL.)* Do you know the de Waals? . . . What's become of them? Their daughter Jopie and I are in the same class, Jopie's my best friend.
DUSSEL	They are gone.

Mauthausen. The death camp! *One of the concentration camps in which many Jews died. (See the map on page* v.*)*

42

ANNE	Gone?	
DUSSEL	With all the others.	610
ANNE	Oh, no. Not Jopie!	

(She turns away, in tears. MRS FRANK motions to MARGOT to comfort her. MARGOT goes to ANNE, putting her arms comfortingly around her.)

MRS VAN DAAN There were some people called Wagner. They lived near us . . .?

MR FRANK *(Interrupting, with a glance at ANNE.)* I think we should put this off until later. We all have many questions we want to ask . . . But I'm sure that Mr Dussel would like to get settled before supper. 620

DUSSEL Thank you. I would, I brought very little with me.

MR FRANK *(Giving him his hat and briefcase.)* I'm sorry we can't give you a room alone. But I hope you won't be too uncomfortable. We've had to make strict rules here . . . a schedule of hours . . . We'll tell you after supper. Anne, would you like to take Mr Dussel to his room?

ANNE *(Controlling her tears.)* If you'll come with me Mr Dussel?

(She starts for her room.)

DUSSEL *(Shaking hands with each in turn.)* Forgive me if I haven't really expressed my gratitude to all of you. This has been 630 such a shock to me. I'd always thought of myself as Dutch. I was born in Holland. My father was born in Holland, and my grandfather. And now . . . after all these years . . . *(He breaks off.)* If you'll excuse me.

(DUSSEL gives a little bow and hurries off after ANNE. MR FRANK and the others are subdued.)

ANNE *(Turning on the light.)* Well, here we are.

(DUSSEL looks around the room. In the main room MARGOT speaks to her mother.)

MARGOT	The news sounds pretty bad, doesn't it? It's so different from what Mr Kraler tells us. Mr Kraler says things are improving.
MR VAN DAAN	I like it better the way Kraler tells it.

(They resume their occupations, quietly. Peter goes off into his room. In ANNE'S room, ANNE turns to DUSSEL.)

ANNE	You're going to share the room with me.
DUSSEL	I'm a man who's always lived alone. I haven't had to adjust myself to others. I hope you'll bear with me until I learn.
ANNE	Let me help you. *(She takes his briefcase.)* Do you always live all alone? Have you no family at all?
DUSSEL	No one.

(He opens his medicine case and spreads his bottles on the dressing table.)

ANNE	How dreadful. You must be terribly lonely.
DUSSEL	I'm used to it.
ANNE	I don't think I could ever get used to it. Didn't you even have a pet? A cat, or a dog?
DUSSEL	I have an allergy for fur-bearing animals. They give me asthma.
ANNE	Oh, dear. Peter has a cat.
DUSSEL	Here? He has it here?
ANNE	Yes. But we hardly ever see it. He keeps it in his room all the time. I'm sure it will be all right.
DUSSEL	Let us hope so.

64

65

66

I have an allergy . . . *Some people have a very bad reaction to cats and other furry animals. In Mr Dussel's case, he can suffer an asthma attack and breathing becomes very difficult.*

(He takes some pills to fortify himself.)

ANNE
That's Margot's bed, where you're going to sleep. I sleep on the sofa there. *(Indicating the clothes hooks on the wall.)* We cleared these off for your things. *(She goes over to the window.)* The best part about this room . . . you can look down and see a bit of the street and the canal. There's a houseboat . . . you can see the end of it . . . a bargeman lives there with his family . . . They have a baby and he's just beginning to walk and I'm so afraid he's going to fall into the canal some day. I watch him . . .

670

DUSSEL
(Interrupting.) Your father spoke of a schedule.

ANNE
(Coming away from the window.) Oh, yes. It's mostly about the times we have to be quiet. And times for the W.C. You can use it now if you like.

DUSSEL
(Stiffly.) No, thank you.

ANNE
I suppose you think its awful, my talking about a thing like that. But you don't know how important it can get to be, especially when you're frightened . . . About this room, the way Margot and I did . . . She had it to herself in the afternoons for studying, reading . . . lessons, you know . . . and I took the mornings. Would that be all right with you?

680

DUSSEL
I'm not at my best in the morning.

ANNE
You stay here in the mornings then. I'll take the room in the afternoon.

DUSSEL
Tell me, when you're in here, what happens to me? Where am I spending my time? In there, with all the people?

690

ANNE
Yes.

DUSSEL
I see. I see.

ANNE
We have supper at half past six.

DUSSEL
(Going over to the sofa.) Then, if you don't mind . . . I like to lie down quietly for ten minutes before eating. I find it

helps the digestion.

ANNE Of course. I hope I'm not going to be too much of a bother to you. I seem to be able to get everyone's back up.

(DUSSEL lies down on the sofa, curled up, his back to her.)

DUSSEL I always get along very well with children. My patients all bring their children to me, because they know I get on well with them. So don't you worry about that. 700

(ANNE leans over him, taking his hand and shaking it gratefully.)

ANNE Thank you. Thank you, Mr Dussel.

(The lights dim to darkness. The curtain falls on the scene. ANNE'S voice comes to us faintly at first, and then with increasing power.)

ANNE'S VOICE . . . And yesterday I finished Cissy Van Marxvelt's latest book. I think she is a first-class writer. I shall definitely let my children read her. 710

Monday the twenty-first of September, nineteen forty-two. Mr Dussel and I had another battle yesterday. Yes, Mr Dussel! According to him, nothing, I repeat . . . nothing, is right about me . . . my appearance, my character, my manners. While he was going on at me I thought . . . sometime I'll give you such a smack that you'll fly right up to the ceiling! Why is it that every grown-up thinks he knows the way to bring up children? Particularly the grown-ups that never had any. I keep wishing that Peter 720 was a girl instead of a boy. Then I would have someone to talk to. Margot's a darling, but she takes everything too seriously.

Cissy Van Marxvelt *A popular Dutch children's writer.*

To pause for a moment on the subject of Mrs Van Daan. I must tell you that her attempts to flirt with Father are getting her nowhere. Pim, thank goodness, won't play.

(As she is saying the last line, the curtain rises on the darkened scene. ANNE'S VOICE fades out.)

WRITING: Suppose Peter kept a diary too. Discuss in pairs what his entry would be for this particular day. Then write out the diary entry.

ACTING: In groups of six, act out the scene from page 28 (where Anne tries on the fur coat) to page 31 (where Mr Van Daan says 'Yes!'.) Bring out how short-tempered Mr Van Daan is becoming.

INTERVIEWING: In pairs, one person takes on the character of Mr Van Daan while the other questions him on the things which irritate him about Anne. (First, read page 33.)

FREEZE-FRAMING: In groups of six, create a 'waxworks tableau' or 'freeze-frame' to represent the moment immediately after Anne has spilt milk on the fur coat. In turn, get each character to say aloud what he/she is thinking.

INTERVIEWING: In pairs, one person takes on the character of Mr Dussel, while the other questions him about his previous life and what he feels about coming to live in the attic with two families.

WRITING: In pairs, discuss what Anne might write in her diary for this day and then write the entry.

DISCUSSION: Imagine you were going to stage a performance of this play. In pairs, discuss and list the props that would be needed for scenes 1, 2 and 3.

WRITING: Imagine you were a pupil at Anne's and Peter's school. Write a letter to a friend who is about to join the school, saying something about each of them.

ACT 1 ❖ SCENE 4

It is the middle of the night, several months later. The stage is dark except for a little light which comes through the skylight in PETER'S room.

Everyone is in bed. MR and MRS FRANK lie on the couch in the main room, which has been pulled out to serve as a makeshift double bed.

MARGOT is sleeping on a mattress on the floor in the main room, behind a curtain stretched across for privacy. The others are all in their accustomed rooms.

From outside we hear two drunken soldiers singing 'Lili Marlene'. A girl's high giggle is heard. The sound of running feet is heard coming closer and then fading in the distance. Throughout the scene there is the distant sound of aeroplanes passing overhead.

A match suddenly flares up in the attic. We dimly see MR VAN DAAN. He is getting his bearings. He comes quickly down the stairs, and goes to the cupboard where the food is stored. Again the match flares up, and is as quickly blown out.

The dim figure is seen to steal back up the stairs.

There is quiet for a second or two, broken only by the sound of aeroplanes, and running feet on the street below.

Suddenly, out of the silence and the dark, we hear ANNE scream.

ANNE	*(Screaming.)* No! No! Don't . . . don't take me!
	(She moans, tossing and crying in her sleep. The other people wake, terrified. DUSSEL sits up in bed, furious.)
DUSSEL	Shush! Anne! Anne, for God's sake, shush!
ANNE	*(Still in her nightmare.)* Save me! Save me!
	(She screams and screams. DUSSEL gets out of bed, going over to her, trying to wake her.)

1

'Lili Marlene' *A popular song with German soldiers during the war, sung by Marlene Dietrich.*

DUSSEL   For God's sake! Quiet! Quiet! You want someone to hear?

                     (In the main room MRS FRANK grabs a shawl and pulls it
                     around her. She rushes in to ANNE, taking her in her arms. MR 10
                     FRANK hurriedly gets up, putting on his overcoat. MARGOT sits
                     up, terrified. PETER'S light goes on in his room.)

MRS FRANK   *(To ANNE, in her room.)* Hush, darling, hush. It's all right.
                     (Over her shoulder to DUSSEL.) Will you be kind enough to
                     turn on the light, Mr Dussel? *(Back to ANNE.)* It's nothing,
                     my darling. It was just a dream.

                     (DUSSEL turns on the light in the bedroom. MRS FRANK holds
                     ANNE in her arms. Gradually ANNE comes out of her
                     nightmare, still trembling with horror. MR FRANK comes into
                     the room, and goes quickly to the window, looking out to be sure 20
                     that no one outside has heard ANNE'S screams. MRS FRANK
                     holds ANNE, talking softly to her. In the main room MARGOT
                     stands on a chair, turning on the centre hanging lamp. A light
                     goes on in the VAN DAAN'S room overhead. PETER puts his
                     robe on, coming out of his room.)

DUSSEL   *(To MRS FRANK, blowing his nose.)* Something must be done
                     about that child, Mrs Frank. Yelling like that! Who knows
                     but there's somebody on the streets? She's endangering our
                     lives.

MRS FRANK   Anne, darling.   30

DUSSEL   Every night she twists and turns. I don't sleep. I spend half
                     my night shushing her. And now it's nightmares!

                     (MARGOT comes to the door of ANNE'S room followed by
                     PETER. MR FRANK goes to them, indicating that everything is
                     all right. PETER takes MARGOT back.)

MRS FRANK   *(To ANNE.)* You're here, safe, you see? Nothing has
                     happéned. *(To DUSSEL)* Please, Mr Dussel, go back to bed.
                     She'll be herself in a minute or two. Won't you, Anne?

DUSSEL   *(Picking up a book and a pillow.)* Thank you, but I'm going to the W.C. The one place where there's peace! 40

(He stalks out. MR VAN DAAN, in underwear and trousers, comes down the stairs.)

MR VAN DAAN *(To DUSSEL.)* What is it? What happened?

DUSSEL A nightmare. She was having a nightmare!

MR VAN DAAN I thought someone was murdering her.

DUSSEL Unfortunately, no.

(He goes into the bathroom. MR VAN DAAN goes back up the stairs. MR FRANK, in the main room, sends PETER back to his own bedroom.)

MR FRANK Thank you, Peter. Go back to bed. 50

(PETER goes back to his room. MR FRANK follows him, turning out the light and looking out the window. Then he goes back to the main room, and gets up on a chair, turning out the centre hanging lamp.)

MRS FRANK *(To ANNE.)* Would you like some water? *(ANNE shakes her head.)* Was it a very bad dream? Perhaps if you told me . . . ?

ANNE I'd rather not talk about it.

MRS FRANK Poor darling. Try to sleep then. I'll sit right here beside you until you fall asleep.

(She brings a stool over, sitting there.) 60

ANNE You don't have to.

MRS FRANK But I'd like to stay with you . . . very much. Really.

ANNE I'd rather you didn't.

MRS FRANK Good night, then. *(She leans down to kiss ANNE. ANNE throws her arm up over her face, turning away. MRS FRANK, hiding her hurt, kisses ANNE'S arm.)* You'll be all right? There's nothing that you want?

ANNE   Will you please ask Father to come.

MRS FRANK   *(After a second.)* Of course, Anne dear. *(She hurries out into the other room. MR FRANK comes to her as she comes in.)* Sie verlangt nach Dir!   70

MR FRANK   *(Sensing her hurt.)* Edith, Liebe, schau . . .

MRS FRANK   Es macht nichts! Ich danke dem lieben Herrgott, dass sie sich wenigstens an Dich wendet, wenn sie Trost braucht! Geh hinein, Otto, sie ist ganz hysterisch vor Angst. *(As MR FRANK hesitates.)* Geh zu ihr. *(He looks at her for a second and then goes to get a cup of water for ANNE. MRS FRANK sinks down on the bed, her face in her hands, trying to keep from sobbing aloud. MARGOT comes over to her, putting her arms around her.)* She wants nothing of me. She pulled away   80
when I leaned down to kiss her.

MARGOT   It's a phase . . . You heard Father . . . Most girls go through it . . . they turn to their fathers at this age . . . they give all their love to their fathers.

MRS FRANK   You weren't like this. You didn't shut me out.

MARGOT   She'll get over it . . .

    (She smoothes the bed for MRS FRANK and sits beside her a moment as MRS FRANK lies down. In ANNE'S room MR FRANK comes in, sitting down by ANNE. ANNE flings her arms around him, clinging to him. In the distance we hear the sound of   90
ack-ack.)

Sie verlangt nach Dir! . . . *When alone, Mr and Mrs Frank still speak German, their mother tongue. Their conversation means:*

MRS FRANK   *She's asking for you.*
MR FRANK   *Edith, darling, look . . .*
MRS FRANK   *It doesn't matter. I thank the dear Lord God that at least she can turn to you when she needs comforting. Go in, Otto, she's quite hysterical with fear. Go to her.*

ANNE	Oh, Pim. I dreamed that they came to get us! The Green Police! They broke down the door and grabbed me and started to drag me out the way they did Jopie.
MR FRANK	I want you to take this pill.
ANNE	What is it?
MR FRANK	Something to quiet you.
	(She takes it and drinks the water. In the main room MARGOT turns out the light and goes back to her bed.)
MR FRANK	*(To ANNE.)* Do you want me to read to you for a while?
ANNE	No. Just sit with me for a minute. Was I awful? Did I yell terribly loud? Do you think anyone outside could have heard?
MR FRANK	No. No. Lie quietly now. Try to sleep.
ANNE	I'm a terrible coward. I'm so disappointed in myself. I think I've conquered my fear . . . I think I'm really grown-up . and then something happens . . . and I run to you like a baby . . . I love you, Father. I don't love anyone but you.
MR FRANK	*(Reproachfully.)* Annele!
ANNE	It's true. I've been thinking about it for a long time. You're the only one I love.
MR FRANK	It's fine to hear you tell me that you love me. But I'd be happier if you said you loved your mother as well . . . She needs your help so much . . . your love . . .
ANNE	We have nothing in common. She doesn't understand me. Whenever I try to explain my views on life to her she asks me if I'm constipated.
MR FRANK	You hurt her very much just now. She's crying. She's in there crying.
ANNE	I can't help it. I only told the truth. I didn't want her

100

110

120

here . . . *(Then, with sudden change.)* Oh Pim, I was horrible,
wasn't I? And the worst of it is, I can stand off and look at
myself doing it and know it's cruel and yet I can't stop
doing it. What's the matter with me? Tell me. Don't say it's
just a phase! Help me.

MR FRANK   There is so little that we parents can do to help our
children. We can only try to set a good example . . . point
the way. The rest you must do yourself. You must build
your own character.

ANNE   I'm trying. Really I am. Every night I think back over all of   130
the things I did that day that were wrong . . . like putting
the wet mop in Mr Dussel's bed . . . and this thing now
with Mother. I say to myself, that was wrong. I make up my
mind, I'm never going to do that again. Never! Of course I
may do something worse . . . but at least I'll never do *that*
again! . . . I have a nicer side, Father . . . a sweeter, nicer
side. But I'm scared to show it. I'm afraid that people are
going to laugh at me if I'm serious. So the mean Anne
comes to the outside and the good Anne stays on the
inside, and I keep on trying to switch them around and   140
have the good Anne outside and the bad Anne inside and
be what I'd like to be . . . and might be . . . if only . . .
only . . .

*(She is asleep. MR FRANK watches her for a moment and then
turns off the light, and starts out. The lights dim out. The
curtain falls on the scene. ANNE'S voice is heard dimly at first,
and then with growing strength.)*

ANNE'S VOICE   The air-raids are getting worse. They come over day and
night. The noise is terrifying. Pim says it should be music to
our ears. The more planes, the sooner will come the end of   150
the war. Mrs Van Daan pretends to be a fatalist. What will
be, will be. But when the planes come over, who is the most
frightened? No one else but Petronella! . . .

Monday, the ninth of November, nineteen forty-two.

Wonderful news! The Allies have landed in Africa. Pim says that we can look for an early finish to the war. Just for fun he asked each of us what was the first thing we wanted to do when we got out of here. Mrs Van Daan longs to be home with her own things, her needle-point chairs, the Beckstein piano her father gave her . . . the best that money could buy. Peter would like to go to a film. Mr Dussel wants to get back to his dentist's drill. He's afraid he is losing his touch. For myself, there are so many things . . . to ride a bike again . . . to laugh till my belly aches . . . to have new clothes from the skin out . . . to have a hot tub filled to overflowing and wallow in it for hours . . . to be back in school with my friends . . .

160

(As the last lines are being said, the curtain rises on the scene. The lights dim on as ANNE'S VOICE fades away.)

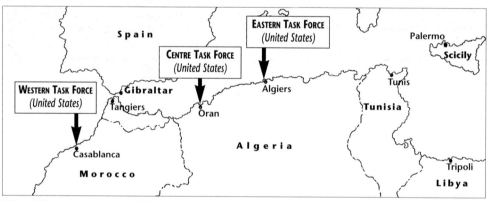

The Allied invasion of Africa, January 1942

STORYBOARDING: If you were making a film of this play, you might decide to show Anne's nightmare. Discuss in pairs what would happen in the nightmare and then storyboard it. The first frame might look like this:

Write notes on what the viewer will hear (e.g. the family screaming, the officer's shouts, Mr Frank calling out to them.)
Write the dialogue on this side, if there is any.

Sketch what the viewer will see.

Write what the camera is doing (e.g. mid-shot of a Gestapo officer arresting Anne's father.)

INTERVIEWING: In pairs, one person takes on the character of Mrs Frank, while the other questions her on how she feels about Anne's behaviour.

WRITING: Pick three of the characters (apart from Anne) and note down what they have learned since they came to live in the attic, and how they have changed.

55

ACT 1 ❖ SCENE 5

It is the first night of the Hanukkah celebration. MR FRANK is standing at the head of the table on which is the Menorah. He lights the Shamos, or servant candle, and holds it as he says the blessing. Seated listening is all of the 'family' dressed in their best. The men wear hats, PETER wears his cap.

MR FRANK *(Reading from a prayer book.)* 'Praised be Thou, oh Lord our   1
God, Ruler of the universe, who has sanctified us with Thy
commandments and bidden us kindle the Hanukkah lights.
Praised be Thou, oh Lord our God, Ruler of the universe,
who has wrought wondrous deliverances for our fathers in
days of old. Praised be Thou, oh Lord our God, Ruler of the
universe, that Thou has given us life and sustenance and
brought us to this happy season.' *(MR FRANK lights the one
candle of the Menorah as he continues.)* 'We kindle this
Hanukkah light to celebrate the great and wonderful deeds   10
wrought through the zeal with which God filled the hearts
of the heroic Maccabees, two thousand years ago. They
fought against indifference, against tyranny and oppression,
and they restored our Temple to us. May these lights
remind us that we should ever look to God, whence cometh
our help.' Amen.

ALL Amen.

(MR FRANK hands MRS FRANK the prayer book.)

MRS FRANK *(Reading.)* 'I lift up mine eyes unto the mountains, from
whence cometh my help. My help cometh from the Lord   20

Hannukah *An eight-day festival of lights that takes place in early December and celebrates the recapture of the temple in Jerusalem by Judas Maccabes in 161 BC. This is a very important celebration on the Jewish calendar. The Menorah is a candelabrum with eight branches and an extra branch for the Shamos, or 'servant candle', used to light the others.*

who made heaven and earth. He will not suffer thy foot to be moved. He that keepeth thee will not slumber. He that keepeth Israel doth neither slumber nor sleep. The Lord is thy keeper. The Lord is thy shade upon thy right hand. The sun shall not smite thee by day, nor the moon by night. The Lord shall keep thee from all evil. He shall keep thy soul. The Lord shall guard thy going out and thy coming in, from this time forth and for evermore.' Amen.

ALL Amen.

(MRS FRANK puts down the prayer book and goes to get the food 30 and wine. MARGOT helps her. MR FRANK takes the men's hats and puts them aside.)

DUSSEL *(Rising.)* That was very moving.

ANNE *(Pulling him back.)* It isn't over yet!

MRS VAN DAAN Sit down! Sit down!

ANNE There's a lot more, songs and presents.

DUSSEL Presents?

MRS FRANK Not this year, unfortunately.

MRS VAN DAAN But always on Hanukkah everyone gives presents . . . everyone! 40

DUSSEL Like our St. Nicholas' Day.

(There is a chorus of 'no's' from the group.)

MRS VAN DAAN No! Not like St. Nicholas! What kind of a Jew are you that you don't know Hanukkah?

MRS FRANK *(As she brings the food.)* I remember particularly the candles . . . First one, as we have tonight. Then the second night you light two candles, the next night three . . . and so on until you have eight candles burning. When there are eight candles it is truly beautiful.

MRS VAN DAAN And the potato pancakes. 50

MR VAN DAAN	Don't talk about them!
MRS VAN DAAN	I make the best *latkes* you ever tasted!
MRS FRANK	Invite us all next year . . . in your own home.
MR FRANK	God willing.
MARGOT	What I remember best is the presents we used to get when we were little . . . eight days of presents . . . and each day they got better and better.
MRS FRANK	*(Sitting down.)* We are all here, alive. That is present enough.
ANNE	No, it isn't. I've got something . . .
	(She rushes into her room, hurriedly puts on a little hat improvised from the lamp shade, grabs a satchel bulging with parcels and comes running back.)
MRS FRANK	What is it?
ANNE	Presents!
MRS VAN DAAN	Presents!
DUSSEL	Look!
MR VAN DAAN	What's she got on her head?
PETER	A lamp shade!
ANNE	*(She picks out one at random.)* This is for Margot. *(She hands it to MARGOT, pulling her to her feet.)* Read it out loud.
MARGOT	*(Reading.)* 'You have never lost your temper. You never will, I fear, You are so good.

60

70

 latkes *Potato pancakes fried in oil (pronounced* lat-keys*)*

But if you should,
Put all your cross words here.'

(She tears open the package.)

A new crossword puzzle book! Where did you get it?

ANNE   It isn't new. It's one that you've done. But I rubbed it all
out, and if you wait a little and forget, you can do it all   80
over again.

MARGOT   *(Sitting.)* It's wonderful, Anne. Thank you. You'd never know
it wasn't new.

(From outside we hear the sound of a streetcar passing.)

ANNE   *(With another gift.)* Mrs Van Daan.

MRS VAN DAAN   *(Taking it.)* This is awful . . . I haven't anything for
anyone . . . I never thought . . .

MR FRANK   This is all Anne's idea.

MRS VAN DAAN   *(Holding up a bottle.)* What is it?

ANNE   It's hair shampoo. I took all the odds and ends of soap and   90
mixed them with the last of my toilet water.

MRS VAN DAAN   Oh, Anneke!

ANNE   I wanted to write a poem for them all, but I didn't have
time. *(Offering a large box to MR VAN DAAN.)* Yours, Mr Van
Daan, is really something . . . something you want more
than anything. *(As she waits for him to open it.)* Look!
Cigarettes!

MR VAN DAAN   Cigarettes.

ANNE   Two of them! Pim found some old tobacco in the pocket

streetcar *The sounds of trams, ringing their bells were a distinctive part of
Amsterdam life.*

lining of his coat . . . and we made them . . . or rather, Pim   10●
did.

MRS VAN DAAN   Let me see . . . Well, look at that! Light it, Putti! Light it.

(*MR VAN DAAN hesitates.*)

ANNE   It's tobacco, really it is! There's a little fluff in it, but not
much.

(*Everyone watches intently as MR VAN DAAN cautiously lights
it. The cigarette flares up. Everyone laughs.*)

PETER   It works!

MRS VAN DAAN   Look at him.

MR VAN DAAN   (*Spluttering.*) Thank you, Anne. Thank you.   11●

(*ANNE rushes back to her satchel for another present.*)

ANNE   (*Handing her mother a piece of paper.*) For Mother, Hanukkah
greeting.

(*She pulls her mother to her feet.*)

MRS FRANK   (*She reads.*) 'Here's an I.O.U. that I promise to pay. Ten
hours of doing whatever you say. Signed, Anne Frank.'

(*MRS FRANK, touched, takes ANNE into her arms, holding her
close.*)

DUSSEL   (*To Anne.*) Ten hours of doing what you're told? Anything
you're told?   12●

ANNE   That's right.

DUSSEL   You wouldn't want to sell that, Mrs Frank?

MRS FRANK   Never! This is the most precious gift I've ever had!

(*She sits, showing her present to the others. ANNE hurries back
to the satchel and pulls out a scarf that MR FRANK found in the
first scene.*)

ANNE   (*Offering it to her father.*) For Pim.

MR FRANK	Anneke . . . I wasn't supposed to have a present!
	(He takes it, unfolding it and showing the others.)
ANNE	It's a muffler . . . to put round your neck . . . like an ascot, 130 you know. I made it myself out of odds and ends . . . I knitted it in the dark each night, after I'd gone to bed. I'm afraid it looks better in the dark!
MR FRANK	*(Putting it on.)* It's fine. It fits me perfectly. Thank you, Annele.
	(ANNE hands PETER a ball of paper, with a string attached to it.)
ANNE	That's for Mouschi.
PETER	*(Rising to bow.)* On behalf of Mouschi, I thank you.
ANNE	*(Hesitant, handing him a gift.)* And . . . this is yours . . . from 140 Mrs Quack Quack. *(As he holds it gingerly in his hands.)* Well . . . open it . . . Aren't you going to open it?
PETER	I'm scared to. I know something's going to jump out and hit me.
ANNE	No. It's nothing like that, really.
MRS VAN DAAN	*(As he is opening it.)* What is it, Peter? Go on. Show it.
ANNE	*(Excitedly.)* It's a safety razor!
DUSSEL	A what?
ANNE	A razor!
MRS VAN DAAN	*(Looking at it.)* You didn't make that out of odds and ends. 150
ANNE	*(To PETER.)* Miep got it for me. It's not new. It's

---

an ascot *A kind of scarf.*

secondhand. But you really do need a razor now.

DUSSEL   For what?

ANNE   Look on his upper lip . . . you can see the beginning of a moustache.

DUSSEL   He wants to get rid of that? Put a little milk on it and let the cat lick if off.

PETER   *(Starting for his room.)* Think you're funny, don't you.

DUSSEL   Look! He can't wait! He's going in to try it!

PETER   I'm going to give Mouschi his present!   16(

(He goes into his room, slamming the door behind him.)

MR VAN DAAN   *(Disgustedly.)* Mouschi, Mouschi, Mouschi.

(In the distance we hear a dog persistently barking. ANNE brings a gift to DUSSEL.)

ANNE   And last but never least, my room-mate, Mr Dussel.

DUSSEL   For me? You have something for me?

(He opens the small box she gives him.)

ANNE   I made them myself.

DUSSEL   *(Puzzled.)* Capsules! Two capsules!

ANNE   They're ear-plugs!   17(

DUSSEL   Ear-plugs?

ANNE   To put in your ears so you won't hear me when I thrash around at night. I saw them advertised in a magazine. They're not real ones . . . I made them out of cotton and candle wax. Try them . . . See if they don't work . . . see if you can hear me talk . . .

DUSSEL   *(Putting them in his ears.)* Wait now until I get them in . . . so.

ANNE	Are you ready?
DUSSEL	Huh? 180
ANNE	Are you ready?
DUSSEL	Good God, they've gone inside! I can't get them out! *(They laugh as MR DUSSEL jumps about, trying to shake the plugs out of his ears. Finally he gets them out. Putting them away.)* Thank you, Anne! Thank you!
MR VAN DAAN	A real Hanukkah
MRS VAN DAAN	Wasn't it cute of her?
MRS FRANK	I don't know when she did it.
MARGOT	I love my present.

Together

ANNE	*(Sitting at the table.)* And now let's have the song, Father . . . 190 please . . . *(To DUSSEL)* Have you heard the Hanukkah song, Mr Dussel? The song is the whole thing! *(She sings.)* 'Oh, Hanukkah! Oh Hanukkah! The sweet celebration . . . '
MR FRANK	*(Quieting her.)* I'm afraid, Anne, we shouldn't sing that song tonight. *(To DUSSEL.)* It's a song of jubilation, of rejoicing. One is apt to become too enthusiastic.
ANNE	Oh, please, please. Let's sing the song. I promise not to shout!
MR FRANK	Very well. But quietly now . . . I'll keep an eye on you and when . . . 200

(As ANNE starts to sing, she is interrupted by DUSSEL, who is snorting and wheezing.)

DUSSEL	*(Pointing to PETER.)* You . . . You! *(PETER is coming from his bedroom, ostentatiously holding a bulge in his coat as if he were*

a song of jubilation, or rejoicing *Because Hannukah celebrated a victory, Mr Frank thinks that the song is inappropriate, given the circumstances of the Jews at that time.*

holding his cat, and dangling ANNE'S present before it.) How many times . . . I told you . . . Out! Out!

MR VAN DAAN *(Going to Peter.)* What's the matter with you? Haven't you any sense. Get that cat out of here.

PETER *(Innocently.)* Cat?

MR VAN DAAN You heard me. Get it out of here!   21(

PETER I have no cat.

(Delighted with his joke, he opens his coat and pulls out a bath towel. The group at the table laugh, enjoying the joke.)

DUSSEL *(Still wheezing.)* It doesn't need to be the cat . . . his clothes are enough . . . when he comes out of that room . . .

MR VAN DAAN Don't worry. You won't be bothered any more. We're getting rid of it.

DUSSEL At last you listen to me.

(He goes off to his bedroom.)

MR VAN DAAN *(Calling after him.)* I'm not doing it for you. That's all in   22(
your mind . . . all of it! *(He starts back to his place at the table.)* I'm doing it because I'm sick of seeing that cat eat all our food.

PETER That's not true. I only give him bones . . . scraps . . .

MR VAN DAAN Don't tell me. He gets fatter every day! Damn cat looks better than any of us. Out he goes tonight!

PETER No! No!

ANNE Mr Van Daan, you can't do that! That's Peter's cat. Peter loves that cat.

MRS FRANK *(Quietly.)* Anne.   23(

PETER *(To MR VAN DAAN.)* If he goes, I go.

MR VAN DAAN Go! Go!

MRS VAN DAAN	You're not going and the cat's not going! Now please . . . this is Hanukkah . . . Hanukkah . . . this is the time to celebrate . . . What's the matter with all of you? Come one, Anne. Let's have the song.
ANNE	*(Singing.)* 'Oh, Hanukkah! Oh Hanukkah! The sweet celebration.'
MR FRANK	*(Rising.)* I think we should first blow out the candle . . . then we'll have something for tomorrow night.
MARGOT	But, Father, you're supposed to let it burn itself out.
MR FRANK	I'm sure that God understands shortages. *(Before blowing it out.)* 'Praised be Thou, oh Lord our God, who hast sustained us and permitted us to celebrate this joyous festival.'
	(He is about to blow out the candle when suddenly there is a crash of something falling below. They all freeze in horror, motionless. For a few seconds there is complete silence. MR FRANK slips off his shoes. The other noiselessly follow his example. MR FRANK turns out a light near him. He motions to PETER to turn off the centre lamp. PETER tries to reach it, realises he cannot and gets up on a chair. Just as he is touching the lamp he loses his balance. The chair goes out from under him. He falls, The iron lamp shade crashes to the floor. There is a sound of feet below, running down the stairs.)
MR VAN DAAN	*(Under his breath.)* God Almighty! *(The only light left comes from the Hanukkah candle. DUSSEL comes from his room. MR FRANK creeps over to the stair-well and stands listening. The dog is heard barking excitedly.)* Do you hear anything?
MR FRANK	*(In a whisper.)* No I think they've gone.
MRS VAN DAAN	It's the Green Police. They've found us.
MR FRANK	If they had, they wouldn't have left. They'd be up here by now.
MRS VAN DAAN	I know it's the Green Police. They've gone to get help. That's all. They'll be back!

240

250

260

65

MR VAN DAAN	Or it may have been the Gestapo, looking for papers . . .
MR FRANK	*(Interrupting.)* Or a thief, looking for money.
MRS VAN DAAN	We've got to do something . . . Quick! Quick! Before they come back.
MR VAN DAAN	There isn't anything to do. Just wait.
	(MR FRANK holds up his hand for them to be quiet. He is listening intently. There is complete silence as they all strain to hear any sound from below. Suddenly ANNE begins to sway. With a low cry she falls to the floor in a faint. MRS FRANK goes to her quickly, sitting beside her on the floor and taking her in her arms.)
MRS FRANK	Get some water, please! Get some water!
	(MARGOT starts for the sink.)
MR VAN DAAN	*(Grabbing MARGOT.)* No! No! No one's going to run water!
MR FRANK	If they've found us, they've found us. Get the water. *(MARGOT starts again for the sink. MR FRANK, getting a flashlight.)* I'm going down.
	(MARGOT rushes to him, clinging to him. ANNE struggles to consciousness.)
MARGOT	No, Father, no! There may be someone there, waiting . . . It may be a trap!
MR FRANK	This is Saturday. There is no way for us to know what has happened until Miep or Mr Kraler comes on Monday morning. We cannot live with this uncertainty.
MARGOT	Don't go, Father!
MRS FRANK	Hush, darling, hush. *(MR FRANK slips quietly out, down the steps and out through the door below.)* Margot! Stay close to me.
	(MARGOT goes to her mother.)

270

280

290

MR VAN DAAN	Shush! Shush!
	(MRS FRANK whispers to MARGOT to get the water. MARGOT goes for it.)
MRS VAN DAAN	Putti, where's our money? Get our money. I hear you can buy the Green Police off, so much a head. Go upstairs quick! Get the money! 300
MR VAN DAAN	Keep still!
MRS VAN DAAN	*(Kneeling before him, pleading.)* Do you want to be dragged off to a concentration camp? Are you going to stand there and wait for them to come up and get you? Do something, I tell you!
MR VAN DAAN	*(Pushing her aside.)* Will you keep still!
	(He goes over to the stair-well to listen. PETER goes to his mother, helping her up on to the sofa. There is a second of silence, then ANNE can stand it no longer.)
ANNE	Someone go after Father! Make Father come back! 310
PETER	*(Starting for the door.)* I'll go.
MR VAN DAAN	Haven't you done enough?
	(He pushes PETER roughly away. In his anger against his father PETER grabs a chair as if to hit him with it, then puts it down, burying his face in his hands. MRS FRANK begins to pray softly.)
ANNE	Please, Please, Mr Van Daan. Get Father.
MR VAN DAAN	Quiet! Quiet!
	(ANNE is shocked into silence. MRS FRANK pulls her closer, holding her protectively in her arms.)
MRS FRANK	*(Softly praying.)* 'I lift up mine eyes unto the mountains, from whence cometh my help. My help cometh from the Lord who made heaven and earth. He will not suffer thy foot to be moved . . . He that keepeth thee will not slumber . . . ' 320

67

(She stops as she hears someone coming. They all watch the door tensely. MR FRANK comes quietly in. ANNE rushes to him, holding him tight.)

MR FRANK   It was a thief. That noise must have scared him away.

MRS VAN DAAN   Thank God.   330

MR FRANK   He took the cash box. And the radio. He ran away in such a hurry that he didn't stop to shut the street door. It was swinging wide open. *(A breath of relief sweeps over them.)* I think it would be good to have some light.

MARGOT   Are you sure it's all right?

MR FRANK   The danger has passed. *(MARGOT goes to light the small lamp.)* Don't be so terrified, Anne. We're safe.

DUSSEL   Who says the danger has passed? Don't you realise we are in greater danger than ever?

MR FRANK   Mr Dussel, will you be still!   340

(MR FRANK takes ANNE back to the table, making her sit down with him, trying to calm her.)

DUSSEL   *(Pointing to PETER.)* Thanks to this clumsy fool, there's someone now who knows we're up here! Someone now knows we're up here, hiding!

MRS VAN DAAN   *(Going to DUSSEL.)* Someone knows we're here, yes. But who is the someone? A thief! A thief! You think a thief is going to go to the Green Police and say . . . I was robbing a place the other night and I heard a noise up over my head? You think a thief is going to do that?   350

DUSSEL   Yes. I think he will.

MRS VAN DAAN   *(Hysterically.)* You're crazy.

(She stumbles back to her seat at the table. PETER follows protectively, pushing DUSSEL aside.)

DUSSEL   I think some day he'll be caught and then he'll make a bargain with the Green Police . . . if they'll let him off, he'll tell them where some Jews are hiding!

(He goes off into the bedroom. There is a second of appalled silence.)

MR VAN DAAN   He's right.   360

ANNE   Father, let's get out of here! We can't stay here now . . . Let's go . . .

MR VAN DAAN   Go! Where?

MRS FRANK   *(Sinking into her chair at the table.)* Yes. Where?

MR FRANK   *(Rising, to them all.)* Have we lost faith? All courage? A moment ago we thought that they'd come for us. We were sure it was the end. But it wasn't the end. We're alive, safe. *(MR VAN DAAN goes to the table and sits. MR FRANK prays.)* 'We thank Thee, oh Lord our God, that in Thy infinite mercy Thou hast again seen fit to spare us.' *(He blows out   370 the candle, then turns to ANNE.)* Come on, Anne. The song! Let's have the song! *(He starts to sing. ANNE finally starts falteringly to sing, as MR FRANK urges her on. Her voice is hardly audible at first.)*

ANNE   *(Singing)* 'Oh Hanukkah! Oh, Hanukkah!

The sweet . . . celebration . . .'

(As she goes on singing, the others gradually join in, their voices still shaking with fear. MRS VAN DAAN sobs as she sings.)

GROUP   'Around the feast . . . we . . . gather
In complete . . . jubilation . . .   380
Happiest of sea . . . sons
Now is here.
Many are the reasons for good cheer.'

(DUSSEL comes from the bedroom. He comes over to the table, standing beside MARGOT, listening to them as they sing.)

'Together

We'll weather
Whatever tomorrow may bring.'

(As they sing on with growing courage, the lights start to dim.)

'So hear us rejoicing
and merrily voicing
The Hanukkah song that we sing.
Hoy!

(The lights are out. The curtain starts slowly to fall.)

'Hear us rejoicing
And merrily voicing
The Hanukkah song that we sing.'

(They are still singing, as the curtain falls.)

Curtain

390

FREEZE-FRAMING: In groups of eight, create a freeze-frame to represent a moment when Mrs Frank was reading (page 57).

DISCUSSION: In pairs, discuss how carefully Anne has thought about Margot's and Mrs Van Daan's presents. How is each one ideal?

DISCUSSION: Read from pages 58 to 63 where Mr Dussel is given his present and discuss as a class the different ways in which each person will have appreciated the present they have received. Who was most touched, do you think?

ACTING: In groups of eight, act out pages 64 to 67, bringing out the tension created by Mr Dussel's reaction to the cat and then the terror at hearing the noise. Discuss the different way in which each character reacts.

DISCUSSION: As a class, discuss why you think the Franks feel it important to celebrate Hanukkah and, particularly, why Mrs Franks's reading was so fitting.

HOT-SEATING: As a class, hot-seat Mr Frank. Ask him very direct questions to get him to reveal his true feelings. (Does he still think it was right to have invited the Van Daans, for example?)

WRITING: Go back to your character dossiers and up-date them, showing how the characters have changed.

ACT 2 ❖ SCENE 1

In the darkness we hear ANNE'S voice, again reading from the diary.

ANNE'S VOICE   Saturday, the first of January, nineteen forty-four. Another   1
new year has begun and we find ourselves still in our
hiding place. We have been here now for one year, five
months and twenty-five days. It seems that our life is at a
standstill . . .

*The curtain rises on the scene. It is late afternoon. Everyone is bundled up against the
cold. In the main room MRS FRANK is taking down the laundry which is hung across
the back. MR FRANK sits in the chair down left, reading. MARGOT is lying on the
couch with a blanket over her and the many coloured knitted scarf around her throat.
ANNE is seated at the centre table, writing in her diary. PETER, MR and MRS VAN*   10
DAAN and DUSSEL are all in their own rooms, reading or lying down.

As the lights dim on, ANNE'S VOICE continues, without a break.

We are all a little thinner. The Van Daans's 'discussions' are
as violent as ever. Mother still does not understand me. But
then I don't understand her either. There is one great
change, however. A change in myself. I read somewhere
that girls of my age don't feel quite certain of themselves.
That they become quiet within and begin to think of the
miracle that is taking place in their bodies. I think that
what is happening to me is so wonderful . . . not only what   20
can be seen, but what is taking place inside. Each time it
has happened I have a feeling that I have a sweet secret.
*(We hear the chimes and then a hymn being played on the
carillon outside.)* And in spite of any pain, I long for the time
when I shall feel that secret within me again.

*(The buzzer of the door below suddenly sounds. Everyone is
startled. MR FRANK tiptoes cautiously to the top of the steps*

and listens. Again the buzzer sounds, in MIEP'S V-for-Victory signal.)

MR FRANK   It's Miep!   3(

(He goes quickly down the steps to unbolt the door. MRS FRANK calls upstairs to the VAN DAANS and then to PETER.)

MRS FRANK   Wake up, everyone! Miep is here! *(ANNE quickly puts her diary away. MARGOT sits up, pulling the blanket around her shoulders. MR DUSSEL sits on the edge of his bed, listening, disgruntled. MIEP comes up the steps, followed by MR KRALER. They bring flowers, books, newspapers, etc. ANNE rushes to MIEP, throwing her arms affectionately around her.)* Miep . . . *and* Mr Kraler . . . What a delightful surprise!

MR KRALER   We came to bring you New Year's greetings.   4(

MRS FRANK   You shouldn't . . . you should have at least one day to yourselves.

(She goes quickly to the stove and brings down teacups and tea for all of them.)

ANNE   Don't say that, it's so wonderful to see them! *(Sniffing at MIEP'S coat.)* I can smell the wind and the cold on your clothes.

MIEP   *(Giving her the flowers.)* There you are. *(Then to MARGOT, feeling her forehead.)* How are you, Margot? . . . Feeling any better?   5(

MARGOT   I'm all right.

ANNE   We filled her full of every kind of pill so she won't cough and make a noise.

(She runs into her room to put the flowers in water. MR and MRS

 V-for-victory signal *In morse code, the letter V is represented by three dots and a dash (• • • —.) This became a signal for victory.*

	VAN DAAN come from upstairs. Outside there is the sound of a band playing.)	
MRS VAN DAAN	Well, hello, Miep. Mr Kraler.	
MR KRALER	*(Giving a bouquet of flowers to MRS VAN DAAN.)* With my hope for peace in the New Year.	
PETER	*(Anxiously.)* Miep, have you seen Mouschi. Have you seen him anywhere around?	60
MIEP	I'm sorry, Peter. I asked everyone in the neighbourhood had they seen a grey cat. But they said no.	
	(MRS FRANK gives MIEP a cup of tea. MR FRANK comes up the steps, carrying a small cake on a plate.)	
MR FRANK	Look what Miep's brought for us!	
MRS FRANK	*(Taking it.)* A cake!	
MR VAN DAAN	A cake! *(He pinches MIEP'S cheeks gaily and hurries up to the cupboard.)* I'll get some plates.	
	(DUSSEL, in his room, hastily puts a coat on and starts out to join the others.)	70
MRS FRANK	Thank you, Miepia. You shouldn't have done it. You must have used all of your sugar rations for weeks. *(Giving it to MRS VAN DAAN.)* It's beautiful, isn't it?	
MRS VAN DAAN	It's been ages since I even saw a cake. Not since you brought us one last year. *(Without looking at the cake, to MIEP.)* Remember? Don't you remember, you gave us one on New Year's Day? Just this time last year? I'll never forget it because you had 'Peace in nineteen forty-three' on it. *(She looks at the cake and reads.)* 'Peace in nineteen forty-four!'	80
MIEP	Well, it has to come sometime, you know. *(As DUSSEL comes from his room.)* Hello, Mr Dussel.	
MR KRALER	How are you?	
MR VAN DAAN	*(Bringing plates and a knife.)* Here's the knife, *liefje*. Now, how	

many of us are there?

MIEP None for me, thank you.

MR FRANK Oh, please. You must.

MIEP I couldn't.

MR VAN DAAN Good! That leaves one . . . two . . . three . . . seven of us.

DUSSEL Eight! Eight! It's the same number as it always is! 9

MR VAN DAAN I left Margot out. I take it for granted Margot won't eat any.

ANNE Why shouldn't she!

MRS FRANK I think it won't harm her.

MR VAN DAAN All right! All right! I just didn't want her to start coughing again, that's all.

DUSSEL And please, Mrs Frank should cut the cake.

MR VAN DAAN What's the difference?

MRS VAN DAAN It's not Mrs Frank's cake, is it Miep?
It's for all of us.

} *Together*

DUSSEL Mrs Frank divides things better. 10

MRS VAN DAAN *(Going to DUSSEL.)* What are you trying to say?

MR VAN DAAN Oh, come on! Stop wasting time!

} *Together*

MRS VAN DAAN *(To DUSSEL.)* Don't I always give everybody exactly the same? Don't I?

MR VAN DAAN Forget it, Kerli.

MRS VAN DAAN No. I want an answer! Don't I?

DUSSEL Yes. Yes. Everybody gets exactly the same . . . except Mr Van Daan always gets a little bit more.

(VAN DAAN advances on DUSSEL, the knife still in his hand.)

MR VAN DAAN That's a lie! 11

(DUSSEL retreats before the onslaught of the VAN DAANS.)

MR FRANK Please, please! *(Then to MIEP.)* You see what a little sugar cake does to us? It goes right to our heads!

MR VAN DAAN *(Handing MRS FRANK the knife.)* Here you are, Mrs Frank.

MRS FRANK Thank you. *(Then to MIEP as she goes to the table to cut the cake.)* Are you sure you won't have some?

MIEP *(Drinking her tea.)* No, really, I have to go in a minute.

(The sound of the band fades out in the distance.)

PETER *(To MIEP.)* Maybe Mouschi when back to our house . . . they say cats . . . Do you ever get over there . . . ? I mean . . . do   120
you suppose you could . . . ?

MIEP I'll try, Peter. The first minute I get I'll try. But I'm afraid, with him gone a week . . .

DUSSEL Make up your mind, already someone has had a nice big dinner from that cat!

(PETER is furious, inarticulate. He starts towards DUSSEL as if to hit him. MR FRANK stops him. MRS FRANK speaks quickly to ease the situation.)

MRS FRANK *(To MIEP.)* This is delicious, Miep!

MRS VAN DAAN *(Eating hers.)* Delicious!   130

MR VAN DAAN *(Finishing it in one gulp.)* Dirk's in luck to get a girl who can bake like this!

MIEP *(Putting down her empty teacup.)* I have to run. Dirk's taking me to a party tonight.

ANNE How heavenly! Remember now what everyone is wearing, and what you have to eat and everything, so you can tell us tomorrow.

MIEP I'll give you a full report! Goodbye, everyone!

MR VAN DAAN *(To MIEP.)* Just a minute. There's something I'd like you to do for me. 140

(He hurries off up the stairs to his room.)

MRS VAN DAAN *(Sharply.)* Putti, where are you going? *(She rushes up the stairs after him, calling hysterically.)* What do you want! Putti, what are you going to do?

MIEP *(To PETER.)* What's wrong?

PETER *(His sympathy is with his mother.)* Father says he's going to sell her fur coat. She's crazy about that old fur coat.

DUSSEL Is it possible? Is it possible that anyone is so silly as to worry about a fur coat in times like this?

PETER It's none of your darn business . . . and if you say one more 150 thing . . . I'll, I'll take you and I'll . . . I mean it . . . I'll . . .

(There is a piercing scream from MRS VAN DAAN above. She grabs at the fur coat as MR VAN DAAN is starting downstairs with it.)

MRS VAN DAAN No! No! No! Don't you dare take that! You hear? It's mine! *(Downstairs PETER turns away, embarrassed, miserable.)* My father gave me that! You didn't give it to me. You have no right. Let go of it . . . you hear?

(MR VAN DAAN pulls the coat from her hands and hurries downstairs. MRS VAN DAAN sinks to the floor, sobbing. As 160 MR VAN DAAN comes into the main room the others look away, embarrassed for him.)

MR VAN DAAN *(To MR KRALER.)* Just a little – discussion over the advisability of selling this coat. As I have often reminded Mrs Van Daan, it's very selfish of her to keep it when people outside are in such desperate need of clothing . . . *(He gives the coat to MIEP.)* So if you will please to sell it for us? It should fetch a good price. And by the way, will you get me cigarettes. I don't care what kind they are . . . get all you can. 170

MIEP	It's terribly difficult to get them, Mr Van Daan. But I'll try. Goodbye.
	(She goes. MR FRANK follows her down the steps to bolt the door after her. MRS FRANK gives MR KRALER a cup of tea.)
MRS FRANK	Are you sure you won't have some cake, Mr Kraler?
MR KRALER	I'd better not.
MR VAN DAAN	You're still feeling badly? What does your doctor say?
MR KRALER	I haven't been to him.
MRS FRANK	Now, Mr Kraler! . . .
MR KRALER	*(Sitting at the table.)* Oh, I tried. But you can't get near a 180 doctor these days . . . they're so busy. After weeks I finally managed to get one on the telephone. I told him I'd like an appointment . . . I wasn't feeling very well. You know what he answers . . . over the telephone . . . Stick out your tongue! *(They laugh. He turns to MR FRANK as MR FRANK comes back.)* I have some contracts here . . . I wonder if you'd look over them with me . . .
MR FRANK	*(Putting out his hand.)* Of course.
MR KRALER	*(He rises.)* If we could go downstairs . . . *(MR FRANK starts ahead, MR KRALER speaks to the others.)* Will you forgive us? 190 I won't keep him but a minute.
	(He starts to follow MR FRANK down the steps.)
MARGOT	*(With sudden foreboding.)* What's happened? Something's happened. Hasn't it, Mr Kraler?
	(MR KRALER stops and comes back, trying to reassure MARGOT with a pretence of casualness.)
MR KRALER	No, really. I want your father's advice . . .
MARGOT	Something's gone wrong! I know it!
MR FRANK	*(Coming back, to MR KRALER.)* If it's something that

| | concerns us here, it's better that we all hear it. | 20 |

MR KRALER   (*Turning to him, quietly.*) But . . . the children . . . ?

MR FRANK   What they'd imagine would be worse than any reality.

(*As MR KRALER speaks, they all listen with intense apprehension. MRS VAN DAAN comes down the stairs and sits on the bottom step.*)

MR KRALER   It's a man in the store-room . . . I don't know whether or not you remember him . . . Carl, about fifty, heavy-set, near-sighted . . . He came with us just before you left.

MR FRANK   He was from Utrecht?

MR KRALER   That's the man. A couple of weeks ago, when I was in the store-room, he closed the door and asked me . . . how's Mr Frank? What do you hear from Mr Frank? I told him I only knew there was a rumour that you were in Switzerland. He said he'd heard the rumour too, but he thought I might know something more. I didn't pay any attention to it . . . but then a thing happened yesterday . . . He'd brought some invoices to the office for me to sign. As I was going through them, I looked up. He was standing staring at the bookcase . . . your bookcase. He said he thought he remembered a door there . . . Wasn't there a door there that used to go up to the loft? Then he told me he wanted more money. Twenty guilders more a week.

MR VAN DAAN   Blackmail!

MR FRANK   Twenty guilders? Very modest blackmail.

MR VAN DAAN   That's just the beginning.

DUSSEL   (*Coming to MR FRANK.*) You know what I think. He was the

---

Utrecht *A Dutch city south-east of Amsterdam. Pronounced* oo-trekt.

guilders *Dutch currency. Twenty guilders was not a great deal of money.*

thief who was down there that night. That's how he knows
we're here.

MR FRANK	*(To MR KRALER.)* How was it left? What did you tell him?
MR KRALER	I said I had to think about it. What shall I do? Pay him the money? . . . Take a chance on firing him . . . or what? I don't know.

230

DUSSEL	*(Frantic.)* For God's sake don't fire him! Pay him what he asks . . . keep him here where you can have your eye on him.
MR FRANK	Is it so much that he's asking? What are they paying nowadays?
MR KRALER	He could get it in a war plant. But this isn't a war plant. Mind you, I don't know if he really knows . . . or if he doesn't know.

240

MR FRANK	Offer him half. Then we'll soon find out if it's blackmail or not.
DUSSEL	And if it is? We've got to pay it, haven't we? Anything he asks we've got to pay!
MR FRANK	Let's decide that when the time comes.
MR KRALER	This may be all my imagination. You get to a point, these days, where you suspect everyone and everything. Again and again . . . on some simple look or word, I've found myself . . .
	(The telephone rings in the office below.)

250

MRS VAN DAAN	*(Hurrying to MR KRALER.)* There's the telephone! What does that mean, the telephone ringing on a holiday?

 war plant *A factory which made weapons or other items for the war.*

MR KRALER	That's my wife. I told her I had to go over some papers in my office . . . to call me there when she got out of church. *(He starts out.)* I'll offer him half then. Goodbye . . . we'll hope for the best!
	(The group call their good-byes half-heartedly. MR FRANK follows MR KRALER, to bolt the door below. During the following scene, MR FRANK comes back up and stands listening, disturbed.) 26
DUSSEL	*(To MR VAN DAAN.)* You can thank your son for this . . . smashing the light. I tell you, it's just a question of time now.
	(He goes to the window at the back and stands looking out.)
MARGOT	Sometimes I wish the end would come . . . whatever it is.
MRS FRANK	*(Shocked.)* Margot!
	(ANNE goes to MARGOT, sitting besides her on the couch with her arms around her.)
MARGOT	Then at least we'd know where we were.
MRS FRANK	You should be ashamed of yourself! Talking that way! Think 27 how lucky we are! Think of the thousands dying in the war, every day. Think of the people in concentration camps.
ANNE	*(Interrupting.)* What's the good of that? What's the good of thinking of misery when you're already miserable? That's stupid!
MRS FRANK	Anne!
	(As ANNE goes on raging at her mother, MRS FRANK tries to break in, in an effort to quiet her.)
ANNE	We're young, Margot and Peter and I. You grown-ups have had your chance! But look at us . . . If we begin thinking of 28 all the horror in the world, we're lost! We're trying to hold on to some kind of ideals . . . when everything . . . ideals, hopes . . . everything, are being destroyed! It isn't our fault

that the world is in such a mess! We weren't around when all this started! So don't try to take it out on us!

(She rushes off to her room, slamming the door after her. She picks up a brush from the chest and hurls it to the floor. Then she sits on the couch, trying to control her anger)

MR VAN DAAN   She talks as if we started the war! Did we start the war?

He spots ANNE'S cake. As he starts to take it, PETER anticipates   290
him.

PETER   She left her cake. *(He starts for ANNE'S room with the cake. There is silence in the main room. MRS VAN DAAN goes up to her room, followed by VAN DAAN. DUSSEL stays looking out the window. MR FRANK brings MRS FRANK her cake. She eats it slowly, without relish. MR FRANK takes his cake to MARGOT and sits quietly on the couch beside her. PETER stands in the doorway of ANNE'S darkened room, looking at her, then makes a little movement to let her know he is there. ANNE sits up, quickly, trying to hide the signs of her tears. PETER holds out the*   300
cake to her.) You left this.

ANNE   *(Dully.)* Thanks.

(PETER starts to go out, then comes back.)

PETER   I thought you were fine just now. You know just how to talk to them. You know just how to say it. I'm no good . . . I never can think . . . especially when I'm mad . . . That Dussel . . . when he said that about Mouschi . . . someone eating him . . . all I could think is . . . I wanted to hit him. I wanted to give him such a . . . a . . . that he'd . . . That's   310
what I used to do when there was an argument at school. That's the way I . . . but here . . . And an old man like that . . . it wouldn't be so good.

ANNE   You're making a big mistake about me. I do it all wrong. I say too much. I go too far. I hurt people's feelings . . .

(DUSSEL leaves the window, going to his room.)

PETER	I think you're just fine . . . What I want to say . . . if it wasn't for you around here, I don't know. What I mean . . .
	(PETER is interrupted by DUSSEL'S turning on the light. DUSSEL stands in the doorway, startled to see PETER. PETER advances towards him forbiddingly. DUSSEL backs out of the room. PETER closes the door on him.) 32
ANNE	Do you mean it, Peter? Do you really mean it?
PETER	I said it, didn't I?
ANNE	Thank you, Peter!
	(In the main room MR and MRS FRANK collect the dishes and take them to the sink, washing them. MARGOT lies down again on the couch. DUSSEL, lost, wanders into PETER'S room and takes up a book, starting to read.)
PETER	*(Looking at the photographs on the wall.)* You've quite a collection. 33
ANNE	Wouldn't you like some in your room? I could give you some. Heaven knows you spend enough time in there . . . doing heaven knows what . . .
PETER	It's easier. A fight starts, or an argument . . . I duck in there.
ANNE	You're lucky, having a room to go to. His lordship is always here . . . I hardly ever get a minute alone. When they start in on me, I can't duck away. I have to stand there and take it.
PETER	You gave some of it back just now.
ANNE	I get so mad. They've formed their opinions . . . about everything . . . but we . . . we're still trying to find out . . . We have problems here that no other people our age have ever had. And just as you think you've solved them, something comes along and bang! You have to start all over again. 34
PETER	At least you've got someone you can talk to.

ANNE	Not really. Mother . . . I never discuss anything serious with her. She doesn't understand. Father's all right. We can talk about everything . . . everything but one thing. Mother. He simply won't talk about her. I don't think you can be really 350 intimate with anyone if he holds something back, do you?
PETER	I think your father's fine.
ANNE	Oh, he is, Peter! He is! He's the only one who's ever given me the feeling that I have any sense. But anyway, nothing can take the place of school and play and friends of your own age . . . or near your age . . . can it?
PETER	I suppose you miss your friends and all.
ANNE	It isn't just . . . *(She breaks off, staring up at him for a second.)* Isn't it funny, you and I? Here we've been seeing each other every minute for almost a year and a half, and this is the 360 first time we've ever really talked. It helps a lot to have someone to talk to, don't you think? It helps you let off steam.
PETER	*(Going to the door.)* Well, any time you want to let off steam, you can come into my room.
ANNE	*(Following him.)* I can get up a awful lot of steam. You'll have to be careful how you say that.
PETER	It's all right with me.
ANNE	Do you mean it?
PETER	I said it, didn't I? 370

(He goes out. ANNE stands in her doorway looking after him. As PETER goes to his door he stands for a minute looking back at her. Then he goes into his room. DUSSEL rises as he comes in, and quickly passes him, going out. He starts across for his room. ANNE sees him coming, and pulls her door shut. DUSSEL turns back toward PETER'S room. PETER pulls his door shut. DUSSEL stands there, bewildered, forlorn.)

The scene slowly dims out. The curtain falls on the scene. ANNE'S VOICE comes over in the darkness . . . faintly at first, and then with growing strength.)   38

ANNE'S VOICE   We've had bad news. The people from whom Miep got our ration books have been arrested. So we have had to cut down our food. Out stomachs are so empty that they rumble and make strange noises, all in different keys. Mr Van Daan's is deep and low, like a bass fiddle. Mine is high, whistling like a flute. As we all sit around waiting for supper, it's like an orchestra tuning up. It only needs Toscanini to raise his baton and we'd be off in the Ride of the Valkyries. Monday, the sixth of March, nineteen forty-four. Mr Kraler is in the hospital. It seems he has ulcers.   39
Pim says we are his ulcers. Miep has to run the business and us too.

The Americans have landed on the southern tip of Italy. Father looks for a quick finish to the war. Mr Dussel is waiting every day for the warehouse man to demand more money. Have I been skipping too much from one subject to another? I can't help it. I feel that spring is coming. I feel it in my whole body and soul. I feel utterly confused. I am longing . . . so longing . . . for everything . . . for friends . . . for someone to talk to . . . someone who understands . . .   40
someone young, who feels as I do . . .

(As these last lines are being said, the curtain rises on the scene. The lights dim on. ANNE'S VOICE fades out.)

Toscanini *A famous conductor.* 'The Ride of the Valkyries' *is a very dramatic and loud piece of music by the German composer, Wagner.*

DISCUSSION: Act 2 begins over a year later. As a class, discuss some of the things that will have taken place during that time. What might have got harder and what easier?

HOT-SEATING: In groups of four, one person takes the character of Mr Van Daan while the others question him about his eating habits and, in particular, question him about what he says to Mr Kraler and Miep about the coat and cigarettes (pages 78 and 79.)

IMPROVISATION: In pairs, discuss whether you think the workman Carl was the thief and whether he is blackmailing Mr Kraler. Then improvise the conversation that takes place when Mr Kraler offers him half of what he has asked for.

INTERVIEWING: In groups of four, one person takes on the character of Mrs Van Daan, one Mr Dussel and one Peter. The other person questions them on whether they agree with Anne that she sometimes 'goes too far' and hurts people's feelings.

WRITING: Up-date the dossiers on your three characters.

DISCUSSION: Although this is a serious play, there are moments of humour. In pairs, look back through Act 2 Scene 1 and decide at which moments an audience might laugh, and why. Make notes on your findings.

ACT 2 ❖ SCENE 2

It is evening, after supper. From outside we hear the sound of children playing. The 'grown-ups', with the exception of MR VAN DAAN, are all in the main room. MRS FRANK is doing some mending. MRS VAN DAAN is reading a fashion magazine. MR FRANK is going over business accounts. DUSSEL, in his dentist's jacket, is pacing up and down, impatient to get into his bedroom. MR VAN DAAN is upstairs working on a piece of embroidery in an embroidery frame.

In his room PETER is sitting before the mirror, smoothing his hair. As the scene goes on, he puts on his tie, brushes his coat and puts it on, preparing himself meticulously for a visit from ANNE. On his wall are now hung some of ANNE'S film stars.

In her room ANNE too is getting dressed. She stands before the mirror in her slip, trying various ways of dressing her hair. MARGOT is seated on the sofa, hemming a skirt for ANNE to wear.

In the main room DUSSEL can stand it no longer. He comes over, rapping sharply on the door of his and ANNE'S bedroom.

ANNE
(Calling to him.) No, no, Mr Dussel! I'm not dressed yet. *(DUSSEL walks away, furious, sitting down and burying his head in his hands. ANNE turns to MARGOT.)* How is that? How does that look?

MARGOT
(Glancing at her briefly.) Fine.

ANNE
You didn't even look.

MARGOT
Of course I did. It's fine.

ANNE
Margot, tell me, am I terribly ugly?

MARGOT
Oh, stop fishing.

ANNE
No. No. Tell me.

MARGOT
Of course, you're not. You've got nice eyes . . . and a lot of animation, and . . .

ANNE	A little vague, aren't you?
	(She reaches over and takes a brassière out of MARGOT'S sewing basket. She holds it up to herself, studying the effect in the mirror. Outside, MRS FRANK, feeling sorry for DUSSEL, comes over, knocking at the girl's door.)
MRS FRANK	*(Outside.)* May I come in?
MARGOT	Come in, Mother.
MRS FRANK	*(Shutting the door behind her.)* Mr Dussel's impatient to get in here. 20
ANNE	*(Still with the brassière.)* Heavens, he takes the room for himself the entire day.
MRS FRANK	*(Gently.)* Anne dear, you're not going in again tonight to see Peter?
ANNE	*(Dignified.)* That is my intention.
MRS FRANK	But you've already spent a great deal of time in there today.
ANNE	I was in there exactly twice. Once to get the dictionary, and then three-quarters of an hour before supper.
MRS FRANK	Aren't you afraid of disturbing him? 30
ANNE	Mother, I have some intuition.
MRS FRANK	Then may I ask this much, Anne. Please don't shut the door when you go in.
ANNE	You sound like Mrs Van Daan!
	(She throws the brassière in MARGOT'S sewing basket and picks up her blouse, putting it on.)
MRS FRANK	No. No. I don't mean to suggest anything wrong. I only

 brassière *the original word from which* **bra** *is formed.*

87

wish that you wouldn't expose yourself to criticism . . . that you wouldn't give Mrs Van Daan the opportunity to be unpleasant.

40

ANNE   Mrs Van Daan doesn't need an opportunity to be unpleasant!

MRS FRANK Everyone's on edge, worried about Mr Kraler. This is one more thing . . .

ANNE   I'm sorry, Mother. I'm going to Peter's room. I'm not going to let Petronella Van Daan spoil our friendship.

(*MRS FRANK hesitates for a second, then goes out, closing the door after her. She gets a pack of playing cards and sits at the centre table, playing solitaire. In ANNE'S room MARGOT hands the finished skirt to ANNE. As ANNE is putting it on, MARGOT takes off her high-heeled shoes and stuffs paper in the toes so that Anne can wear them.*)

50

MARGOT   (*To ANNE.*) Why don't you two talk in the main room? It'd save a lot of trouble. It's hard on Mother, having to listen to those remarks from Mrs Van Daan and not say a word.

ANNE   Why doesn't she say a word? I think it's ridiculous to take it and take it.

MARGOT   You don't understand Mother at all, do you? She can't talk back. She's not like you. It's just not in her nature to fight back.

60

ANNE   Anyway . . . the only one I worry about is you. I feel awfully guilty about you.

(*She sits on the stool near MARGOT, putting on MARGOT'S high-heeled shoes.*)

MARGOT   What about?

ANNE   I mean, every time I go into Peter's room, I have a feeling I may be hurting you. (*MARGOT shakes her head.*) I know if it were me, I'd be wild. I'd be desperately jealous, if it were me.

MARGOT	Well, I'm not.	70

ANNE	You don't feel badly? Really? Truly? You're not jealous?

MARGOT	Of course I'm jealous . . . jealous that you've got something to get up in the morning for . . . But jealous of you and Peter? No.

(ANNE goes back to the mirror.)

ANNE	Maybe there's nothing to be jealous of. Maybe he doesn't really like me. Maybe I'm just taking the place of his cat . . . *(She picks up a pair of short white gloves, putting them on.)* Wouldn't you like to come in with us?	
MARGOT	I have a book.	80

(The sound of children playing outside fades out. In the main room DUSSEL can stand it no longer. He jumps up, going to the bedroom door and knocking sharply.)

DUSSEL	Will you please let me in my room!

ANNE	Just a minute, dear, dear Mr Dussel. *(She picks up her mother's pink stole and adjusts it elegantly over her shoulders, then gives a last look in the mirror.)* Well, here I go . . . to run the gauntlet.

(She starts out, followed by MARGOT.)

DUSSEL	*(As she appears – sarcastic.)* Thank you so much.	90

(DUSSEL goes into his room. ANNE goes towards PETER'S room, passing MRS VAN DAAN and her parents at the centre table.)

MRS VAN DAAN	My God, look at her! *(ANNE pays no attention. She knocks at PETER'S door.)* I don't know what good it is to have a son. I never see him. He wouldn't care if I killed myself. *(PETER opens the door and stands aside for ANNE to come in.)* Just a minute, Anne. *(She goes to them at the door.)* I'd like to say a few words to my son. Do you mind? *(PETER and ANNE stand waiting.)* Peter, I don't want you staying up till all hours tonight. You've got to have your sleep. You're a	100

growing boy. You hear?

MRS FRANK Anne won't stay late. She's going to bed promptly at nine. Aren't you, Anne?

ANNE Yes, Mother . . . *(To MRS VAN DAAN.)* May we go now?

MRS VAN DAAN Are you asking me? I didn't know I had anything to say about it.

MRS FRANK Listen for the chimes, Anne dear.

(The two young people go off into PETER'S room, shutting the door after them.)

MRS VAN DAAN *(To MRS FRANK.)* In my day it was the boys who called on the girls. Not the girls on the boys.

MRS FRANK You know how young people like to feel that they have secrets. Peter's room is the only place where they can talk.

MRS VAN DAAN Talk! That's not what they called it when I was young.

(MRS VAN DAAN goes off to the bathroom. MARGOT settles down to read her book. MR FRANK puts his papers away and brings a chess game to the centre table. He and MRS FRANK start to play. In PETER'S room, ANNE speaks to PETER, indignant, humiliated.)

ANNE Aren't they awful? Aren't they impossible? Treating us as if we were still in the nursery.

(She sits on the cot. PETER gets a bottle of lemonade and two glasses.)

PETER Don't let it bother you. It doesn't bother me.

ANNE I suppose you can't really blame them . . . they think back to what *they* were like at our age. They don't realise how much more advanced we are . . . When you think what wonderful discussions we've had! . . . Oh, I forgot. I was going to bring you some more pictures.

PETER Oh, these are fine, thanks.

ANNE	Don't you want some more? Miep just brought me some new ones.
PETER	Maybe later.
	(He gives her a glass of lemonade and, taking some for himself, sits down facing her.)
ANNE	*(Looking up at one of the photographs.)* I remember when I got that . . . I won it. I bet Jopie that I could eat five ice-cream cones. We'd all been playing ping-pong . . . We used to have heavenly times . . . we'd finish up with ice-cream at the Delphi, or the Oasis, where Jews were allowed . . . there'd always be a lot of boys . . . we'd laugh and joke . . . I'd like to go back to it for a few days or a week. But after that I know I'd be bored to death. I think more seriously about life now. I want to be a journalist . . . or something. I love to write. What do you want to do?
PETER	I thought I might go off some place . . . work on a farm or something . . . some job that doesn't take much brains.
ANNE	You shouldn't talk that way. You've got the most awful inferiority complex.
PETER	I know I'm not clever.
ANNE	That isn't true. You're much better than I am in dozens of things . . . arithmetic and algebra and . . . well, you're a million times better than I am at algebra. *(With sudden directness.)* You like Margot, don't you? Right from the start you liked her, liked her much better than me.
PETER	*(Uncomfortably.)* Oh, I don't know.
	(In the main room MRS VAN DAAN comes from the bathroom

140

150

the Delphi, or the Oasis . . . *Cafés which Jews were allowed to use.*

inferiority complex *A belief that you are not as good as everybody else.*

and goes over to the sink, polishing a coffee pot.)

ANNE   It's all right. Everyone feels that way. Margot's so good. She's sweet and bright and beautiful and I'm not.   16

PETER   I wouldn't say that.

ANNE   Oh, no, I'm not. I know that. I know quite well that I'm not a beauty. I never have been and never shall be.

PETER   I don't agree at all. I think you're pretty.

ANNE   That's not true!

PETER   And another thing. You've changed . . . from at first, I mean.

ANNE   I have?

PETER   I used to think you were awfully noisy.

ANNE   And what do you think now, Peter? How have I changed?   17

PETER   Well . . . er . . . you're . . . quieter.

(In his room DUSSEL takes his pyjamas and toilet articles and goes into the bathroom to change.)

ANNE   I'm glad you don't just hate me.

PETER   I never said that.

ANNE   I bet when you get out of here you'll never think of me again.

PETER   That's crazy.

ANNE   When you get back with all of your friends, you're going to say . . . now what did I ever see in that Mrs Quack Quack.   18

PETER   I haven't got any friends.

ANNE   Oh, Peter, of course you have. Everyone has friends.

PETER   Not me. I don't want any. I get along all right without them.

ANNE	Does that mean you can get along without me? I think of myself as your friend.
PETER	No. If they were all like you, it'd be different.
	(He takes the glasses and the bottle and puts them away. There is a second's silence then Anne speaks, hesitantly, shyly.)
ANNE	Peter, did you ever kiss a girl?
PETER	Yes. Once.
ANNE	*(To cover her feelings.)* That picture's crooked. *(PETER goes over, straightening the photograph.)* Was she pretty?
PETER	Huh?
ANNE	The girl that you kissed.
PETER	I don't know. I was blindfolded. *(He comes back and sits down again.)* It was at a party. One of those kissing games.
ANNE	*(Relieved.)* Oh. I don't suppose that really counts, does it?
PETER	It didn't with me.
ANNE	I've been kissed twice. Once a man I'd never seen before kissed me on the cheek when he picked me up off the ice and I was crying. And the other was Mr Koophuis, a friend of Father's who kissed my hand. You wouldn't say those counted, would you?
PETER	I wouldn't say so.
ANNE	I know almost for certain that Margot would never kiss anyone unless she was engaged to them. And I'm sure too that Mother never touched a man before Pim. But I don't know . . . things are so different now . . . What do you think? Do you think a girl shouldn't kiss anyone except if she's engaged or something? It's so hard to try to think what to do, when here we are with the whole world falling around our ears and you think . . . well . . . you don't know what's going to happen tomorrow and . . . What do you think?

190

200

210

PETER	I suppose it'd depend on the girl. Some girls, anything they do's wrong. But others . . . well . . . it wouldn't necessarily be wrong with them. *(The carillon starts to strike nine o'clock.)* I've always thought that when two people . . .
ANNE	Nine o'clock. I have to go.
PETER	That's right.
ANNE	*(Without moving.)* Good night.
	(There is a second's pause, then PETER gets up and moves towards the door.)
PETER	You won't let them stop you coming?
ANNE	No *(She rises and starts for the door.)* Sometime I might bring my diary. There are so many things in it that I want to talk over with you. There's a lot about you.
PETER	What kind of thing?
ANNE	I wouldn't want you to see some of it. I thought you were a nothing, just the way you thought about me.
PETER	Did you change your mind, the way I changed my mind about you?
ANNE	Well . . . You'll see . . .
	(For a second ANNE stands looking up at PETER, longing for him to kiss her. As he makes no move she turns away. Then suddenly PETER grabs her awkwardly in his arms, kissing her on the cheek. ANNE walks out dazed. She stands for a minute, her back to the people in the main room. As she regains her poise she goes to her mother and father and MARGOT, silently kissing them. They murmur their good nights to her. As she is about to open her bedroom door, she catches sight of MRS VAN DAAN. She goes quickly to her, taking her face in her hands and kissing her first on one cheek and then on the other. Then she hurries off into her room. MRS VAN DAAN looks after her, and then looks over at PETER'S room. Her suspicions are confirmed.)

22

23

24

MRS VAN DAAN   *(She knows.)* Ah hah!

(The lights dim out. The curtain falls on the scene. In the darkness ANNE'S voice comes faintly at first and then with growing strength.)   250

ANNE'S VOICE   By this time we all know each other so well that if anyone starts to tell a story, the rest can finish it for him. We're having to cut down still further on our meals. What makes it worse, the rats have been at work again. They've carried off some of our precious food. Even Mr Dussel wishes now that Mouschi was here.

Thursday, the twentieth of April, nineteen forty-four. Invasion fever is mounting every day. Miep tells us that people outside talk of nothing else. For myself, life has become much more pleasant. I often go to Peter's room   260
after supper. Oh, don't think I'm in love, because I'm not. But it does make life more bearable to have someone with whom you can exchange views. No more tonight. P.S. . . . I must be honest. I must confess that I actually live for the next meeting. Is there anything lovelier than to sit under the skylight and feel the sun on your cheeks and have a darling boy in your arms? I admit now that I'm glad the Van Daans had a son and not a daughter. I've outgrown another dress. That's the third. I'm having to wear Margot's clothes after all. I'm working hard on my French and am   270
now reading *La Belle Nivernaise.*

(As she is saying the last line – the curtain rises on the scene. The lights dim on, as ANNE'S VOICE fades out.)

invasion fever *People were becoming excited in the spring of 1944 because there were rumours that the Allies were about to invade the mainland of Europe.*

DISCUSSION: As a class, discuss what Mrs Frank might mean by warning Anne, 'I only wish you wouldn't expose yourself to criticism.' (page 87) What is she worried about and what is Mrs Van Daan angry about on page 89?

DISCUSSION: As a class, discuss whether you agree with Anne that Peter has 'the most awful inferiority complex.' Refer to details in the play to support what you say.

DISCUSSION: By this stage in the story, Anne is nearly 15 and Peter 17 or 18. As a class, discuss the differences between then and now, in the ways young people behave (a) with adults, and (b) with each other.

DISCUSSION: In pairs, reread the conversation between Anne and Peter on pages 90 to 94. Then compare it with Anne's actual diary entry for that day. Discuss as a class what you notice about the ways in which the playwrights have used Anne's private thoughts in order to create a scene that can be acted out.

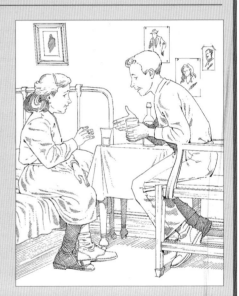

WRITING: Write a second entry in Peter's diary. Make it very different from the first entry, in order to show how some of Peter's attitudes have changed.

ACT 2 ❖ SCENE 3

*It is night, a few weeks later. Everyone is in bed. There is
complete quiet. In the VAN DAAN'S room a match flares up for
a moment and then is quickly put out. MR VAN DAAN, in bare
feet, dressed in underwear and trousers, is dimly seen coming
stealthily down the stairs and into the main room, where MR
and MRS FRANK and MARGOT are sleeping. He goes to the food
safe and again lights a match. Then he cautiously opens the
safe, taking out a half-loaf of bread. As he closes the safe, it
creaks. He stands rigid. MRS FRANK sits up in bed. She sees
him.*

MRS FRANK	*(Screaming.)* Otto! Otto! Komme schnell!	1

(The rest of the people wake, hurriedly getting up.)

MR FRANK   Was ist los? Was ist passiert?

(DUSSEL, followed by ANNE, comes from his room.)

MRS FRANK   *(As she rushes over to MR VAN DAAN.)* Er stiehlt das Essen!

DUSSEL   *(Grabbing MR VAN DAAN.)* You! You! Give me that.

MRS VAN DAAN   *(Coming down the stairs.)* Putti . . . Putti . . . what is it?

DUSSEL   *(His hand on VAN DAAN'S neck.)* You dirty thief . . . stealing
food . . . you good-for-nothing . . .

MR FRANK   Mr Dussel! For God's sake! Help me, Peter!   10

*(PETER comes over, trying, with MR FRANK, to separate the two
struggling men.)*

Komme schnell! . . . MRS FRANK *Otto! Otto! Come here quickly!*
                    MR FRANK *What's the matter? What's happened?*
                    MRS FRANK *He's stealing the food!*

PETER   Let him go! Let go!

(DUSSEL drops MR VAN DAAN, pushing him away. He shows them the end of a loaf of bread that he has taken from VAN DAAN.)

DUSSEL   You greedy, selfish . . . !

(MARGOT turns on the lights.)

MRS VAN DAAN   Putti . . . what is it?

(All of MRS FRANK'S gentleness, her self-control, is gone. She is outraged, in a frenzy of indignation.)   20

MRS FRANK   The bread! He was stealing the bread!

DUSSEL   It was you, and all the time we thought it was the rats!

MR FRANK   Mr Van Daan, how could you!   30

MR VAN DAAN   I'm hungry.

MRS FRANK   We're all of us hungry! I see the children getting thinner and thinner. Your own son Peter . . . I've heard him moan in his sleep, he's so hungry. And you come in the night and steal food that should go to them . . . to the children!

MRS VAN DAAN   *(Going to MR VAN DAAN protectively.)* He needs more food than the rest of us. He's used to more. He's a big man.

(MR VAN DAAN breaks away, going over and sitting on the couch.)   40

MRS FRANK   *(Turning on MRS VAN DAAN.)* And you . . . you're worse than he is!. You're a mother, and yet you sacrifice your child to this man . . . this . . . this . . .

MR FRANK Edith! Edith!

(MARGOT picks up the pink woollen stole, putting it over her mother's shoulders.)

MRS FRANK *(Paying no attention, going on to MRS VAN DAAN.)* Don't think I haven't seen you! Always saving the choicest bits for him! I've watched you day after day and I've held my tongue. But no longer! Not after this! Now I want him to go! I want him to get out of here!

50

MR FRANK Edith!

MR VAN DAAN Get out of here?

} Together

MRS VAN DAAN What do you mean?

MRS FRANK Just that! Take your things and get out!

MR FRANK *(To MRS FRANK.)* You're speaking in anger. You cannot mean what you are saying.

MRS FRANK I mean exactly that!

(MRS VAN DAAN takes a cover from the FRANK'S bed, pulling it about her.)

60

MR FRANK For two long years we have lived here, side by side. We have respected each other's rights . . . we have managed to live in peace. Are we now going to throw it all away? I know this will never happen again, will it, Mr Van Daan?

MR VAN DAAN No. No.

MRS FRANK He steals once! He'll steal again!

(MR VAN DAAN, holding his stomach, starts for the bathroom. ANNE puts her arms around him, helping him up the step.)

MR FRANK Edith, please. Let us be calm. We'll all go to our rooms . . . and afterwards we'll sit down quietly and talk this out . . .

70

we'll find some way . . .

MRS FRANK   No! No! No more talk! I want them to leave!

MRS VAN DAAN   You'd put us out, on the streets?

MRS FRANK   There are other hiding places.

MRS VAN DAAN   A cellar . . . cupboard. I know. And we have no money left
even to pay for that.

MRS FRANK   I'll give you money. Out of my own pocket I'll give it
gladly.

(She gets her purse from a shelf and comes back with it.)   8

MRS VAN DAAN   Mr Frank, you told Putti you'd never forget what he'd done
for you when you came to Amsterdam. You said you could
never repay him, that you . . .

MRS FRANK   *(Counting out money.)* If my husband had any obligation to
you, he's paid it, over and over.

MR FRANK   Edith, I've never seen you like this before. I don't know
you.

MRS FRANK   I should have spoken out long ago.

DUSSEL   You can't be nice to some people.

MRS VAN DAAN   *(turning on DUSSEL.)* There would have been plenty for all of   9
us, if you hadn't come in here!

MR FRANK   We don't need the Nazis to destroy us. We're destroying
ourselves.

*(He sits down, with his head in his hands. MRS FRANK goes to
MRS VAN DAAN.)*

MRS FRANK   *(Giving MRS VAN DAAN some money.)* Give this to Miep.
She'll find you a place.

ANNE   Mother, you're not putting Peter out. Peter hasn't done
anything.

MRS FRANK	He'll stay, of course. When I say I must protect the children, **100** I mean Peter too.
	(PETER rises from the steps where he has been sitting.)
PETER	I'd have to go if Father goes.
	(MR VAN DAAN comes from the bathroom. MRS VAN DAAN hurries to him and takes him to the couch. Then she gets water from the sink to bathe his face.)
MRS FRANK	*(While this is going on.)* He's no father to you . . . that man! He doesn't know what it is to be a father!
PETER	*(Starting for his room.)* I wouldn't feel right. I couldn't stay.
MRS FRANK	Very well, then. I'm sorry. **110**
ANNE	*(Rushing over to PETER.)* No, Peter! No! *(PETER goes into his room, closing the door after him. ANNE turns back to her mother crying.)* I don't care above the food. They can have mine! I don't want it! Only don't send them away. It'll be daylight soon. They'll be caught . . .
MARGOT	*(Putting her arms comfortingly around ANNE.)* Please, Mother!
MRS FRANK	They're not going now. They'll stay here until Miep finds them a place. *(To MRS VAN DAAN.)* But one thing I insist on! He must never come down here again! He must never come to this room where the food is stored! We'll divide **120** what we have . . . an equal share for each! *(DUSSEL hurries over to get a sack of potatoes from the food safe. MRS FRANK goes on, to MRS VAN DAAN.)* You can cook it here and take it up to him.
	(DUSSEL brings the sack of potatoes back to the centre table.)
MARGOT	Oh, no. No. We haven't sunk so far that we're going to fight over a handful of rotten potatoes.
DUSSEL	*(Dividing the potatoes into piles.)*Mrs Frank, Mr Frank, Margot, Anne, Peter, Mrs Van Daan, Mr Van Daan, myself . . . Mrs Frank . . . **130**

101

(The buzzer sounds in MIEP'S signal.)

MR FRANK   It's Miep!

(He hurries over, getting his overcoat and putting it on.)

MARGOT   At this hour?

MRS FRANK   It is trouble.

MR FRANK   *(As he starts down to unbolt the door.)* I beg you, don't let her see a thing like this!

DUSSEL   *(Counting without stopping.)* . . . Anne, Peter, Mrs Van Daan, Mr Van Daan, myself . . .

MARGOT   *(To DUSSEL.)* Stop it! Stop it!   14

DUSSEL   . . . . Mr Frank, Margot, Anne, Peter, Mrs Van Daan, Mr Van Daan, myself, Mrs Frank . . .

MRS VAN DAAN   You're keeping the big ones for yourself! All the big ones . . . Look at the size of that! . . . And that! . . .

(DUSSEL continues on with his dividing. PETER, with his shirt and trousers on, comes from his room.)

MARGOT   Stop it! Stop it!

(We hear MIEP'S excited voice speaking to MR FRANK below.)

MIEP   Mr Frank . . . the most wonderful news! . . . The invasion has begun!   15

MR FRANK   Go on, tell them! Tell them!

(MIEP comes running up the steps, ahead of MR FRANK. She has a man's raincoat on over her night-clothes and a bunch of orange-coloured flowers in her hand.)

The invasion has begun! *The Allies landed on the coast of Normandy (northern France) on 'D-Day', the 6th of June, 1944. BBC radio broadcast the news as well as speeches by the British Prime Minister, Sir Winston Churchill, and the commander of the united Allied forces, General Dwight D Eisenhower.*

MIEP	Did you hear that, everybody? Did you hear what I said? The invasion has begun! The invasion!
	(They all stare at MIEP, unable to grasp what she is telling them. PETER is the first to recover his wits.)
PETER	Where?
MRS VAN DAAN	When? When, Miep?
MIEP	It began early this morning . . .
	(As she talks on, the realisation of what she has said begins to dawn on them. Everyone goes crazy. A wild demonstration takes place. MRS FRANK hugs MR VAN DAAN.)
MRS FRANK	Oh, Mr Van Daan, did you hear that?
	(DUSSEL embraces MRS VAN DAAN. PETER grabs a frying pan and parades around the room, beating on it, singing the Dutch National Anthem. ANNE and MARGOT follow him singing, weaving in and out among the excited grown-ups. MARGOT breaks away to take the flowers from MIEP and distribute them to everyone. While this pandemonium is going on MRS FRANK tries to make herself heard above the excitement.)
MRS FRANK	*(To MIEP.)* How do you know?
MIEP	The radio . . . The B.B.C.! They said they landed on the coast of Normandy!
PETER	The British?
MIEP	British, Americans, French, Dutch, Poles, Norwegians . . . all of them! More than four thousand ships! Churchill spoke, and General Eisenhower! D-Day they call it!
MR FRANK	Thank God, it's come!
MRS VAN DAAN	At last!
MIEP	*(Starting out.)* I'm going to tell Mr Kraler. This'll be better than any blood transfusion.

160

170

180

MR FRANK	*(Stopping her.)* What part of Normandy did they land, did they say?
MIEP	Normandy . . . that's all I know now . . . I'll be up the minute I hear some more!
	(She goes hurriedly out.)
MR FRANK	*(To MRS FRANK.)* What did I tell you? What did I tell you?
	(MRS FRANK indicates that he has forgotten to bolt the door after MIEP. He hurries down the steps. MR VAN DAAN, sitting on the couch, suddenly breaks into a convulsive sob. Everybody looks at him, bewildered.) 19
MRS VAN DAAN	*(Hurrying to him.)* Putti! Putti! What is it? What happened?
MR VAN DAAN	Please. I'm so ashamed.
	(MR FRANK comes back up the steps.)
DUSSEL	Oh, for God's sake!
MRS VAN DAAN	Don't, Putti.
MARGOT	It doesn't matter now!
MR FRANK	*(Going to MR VAN DAAN.)* Didn't you hear what Miep said? 20 The invasion has come! We're going to be liberated! This is a time to celebrate!
	(He embraces MRS FRANK and then hurries to the cupboard and gets the cognac and a glass.)
MR VAN DAAN	To steal bread from children!
MRS FRANK	We've all done things that we're ashamed of.
ANNE	Look at me, the way I've treated Mother . . . so mean and horrid to her.

  liberated *'set free from Nazi rule'*

MRS FRANK	No, Anneke, no.
	(ANNE runs to her mother, putting her arms around her.) 210
ANNE	Oh, Mother, I was awful.
MR VAN DAAN	Not like me. No one is as bad as me!
DUSSEL	*(To MR VAN DAAN.)* Stop it now! Let's be happy!
MR FRANK	*(Giving MR VAN DAAN a glass of cognac.)* Here! Here! Schnapps! Lochein!
	(VAN DAAN takes the cognac. They all watch him. He gives them a feeble smile. ANNE puts up her fingers in a V-for-Victory sign. As VAN DAAN gives an answering V-sign, they are startled to hear a loud sob from behind them. It is MRS FRANK, stricken with remorse. She is sitting on the other side of the room.) 220
MRS FRANK	*(Through her sobs.)* When I think of the terrible things I said . . .
	(MR FRANK, ANNE and MARGOT hurry to her, trying to comfort her. MR VAN DAAN brings her his glass of cognac.)
MR VAN DAAN	No! No! You were right!
MRS FRANK	That I should speak that way to you! . . . Our friends! . . . Our guests!
	(She starts to cry again.)
DUSSEL	Stop it, you're spoiling the whole invasion!
	(As they are comforting her, the lights dim out. The curtain falls.) 230

Schnapps! Locheim! *'Cheers! Good health!'* Locheim literally means: *'To life!'*

V-for-Victory sign This sign (in which a V shape is made with the fingers with the palm of the hand outwards) was made famous by Winston Churchill.

stricken with remorse Mrs Frank is overcome with regret and guilt for what she has just said to Mr Van Daan.

ANNE'S VOICE   *(Faintly at first and then with growing strength.)* We're all in much better spirits these days. There's still excellent news of the invasion. The best part about it is that I have a feeling that friends are coming. Who knows? Maybe I'll be back in school by fall. Ha, ha! The joke is on us! The warehouse man doesn't know a thing and we are paying him all that money! . . .

Wednesday, the second of July, nineteen forty-four. The invasion seems temporarily to be bogged down. Mr Kraler has to have an operation, which looks bad. The Gestapo have found the radio that was stolen. Mr Dussel says they'll trace it back and back to the thief, and then, it's just a matter of time till they get to us. Everyone is low. Even poor Pim can't raise their spirits. I have often been downcast myself . . . but never in despair. I can shake off everything if I write. But . . . and that is the great question . . . will I ever be able to write well? I want to so much. I want to go on living even after my death. Another birthday has gone by, so now I am fifteen. Already I know what I want. I have a goal, an opinion.

(As this is being said – the curtain rises on the scene, the lights dim on, and ANNE'S VOICE fades out.)

Gestapo *The Nazi secret police whose role was to suppress 'political crimes'.*

I want to go on living . . . *In a sense, this is what has happened to Anne Frank, who continues to live on through her diary.*

FREEZE-FRAMING: In groups of eight, create a tableau to represent any moment during the discovery of Mr Van Daan's attempted raid on the food. In turn, ask each character to say aloud what he/she is thinking.

DISCUSSION: Mr Frank says, 'We don't need the Nazis to destroy us. We're destroying ourselves.' As a class, discuss how the following people's behaviour is destructive at this point: Mrs Frank, Mr Van Daan and Mr Dussel. Then consider which strong qualities are shown in the quiet Margot. Refer closely to the script to illustrate the points you make.

DISCUSSION: As a class, discuss whether you have any sympathy for Mr Van Daan.

ARTWORK: In pairs, discuss how Anne's feelings change from the beginning of the scene to the end. Draw a graph, with 'happiness' on the *y* axis (10 for very happy, 0 for very unhappy) and the different moments of the scene on the *x* axis. When you have finished, compare it with other people's.

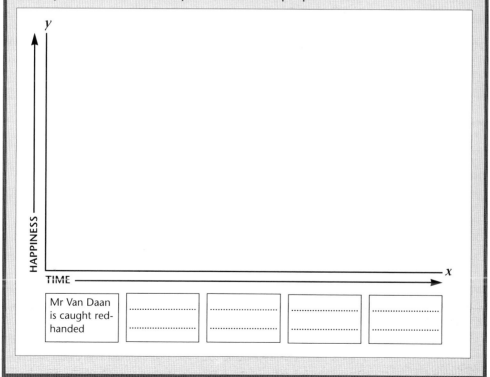

ACT 2 ❖ SCENE 4

It is an afternoon a few weeks later . . . Everyone but MARGOT is in the main room. There is a sense of great tension.

Both MRS FRANK and MR VAN DAAN are nervously pacing back and forth. DUSSEL is standing at the window, looking down fixedly at the street below. PETER is at the centre table, trying to do his lessons. ANNE sits opposite him, writing her diary. MRS VAN DAAN is seated on the couch, her eyes on MR FRANK as he sits reading

The sound of a telephone ringing comes from the office below. They are all rigid, listening tensely. DUSSEL rushes down to MR FRANK.

DUSSEL	There it goes again, the telephone! Mr Frank, do you hear?
MR FRANK	*(Quietly.)* Yes. I hear.
DUSSEL	*(Pleading, insistent.)* But this is the third time, Mr Frank! The third time in quick succession! It's a signal! I tell you it's Miep, trying to get us! For some reason she can't come to us and she's trying to warn us of something!
MR FRANK	Please. Please.
MR VAN DAAN	*(To DUSSEL.)* You're wasting your breath.
DUSSEL	Something has happened, Mr Frank. For three days now Miep hasn't been to see us! And today not a man has come to work. There hasn't been a sound in the building!
MRS FRANK	Perhaps it's Sunday. We may have lost track of the days.
MR VAN DAAN	*(To ANNE.)* You with the diary there. What day is it?
DUSSEL	*(Going to MRS FRANK.)* I don't lose track of the days! I know exactly what day it is! It's Friday, the fourth of August. Friday, and not a man at work. *(He rushes back to MR FRANK, pleading with him, almost in tears.)* I tell you Mr Kraler's dead. That's the only explanation. He's dead and they've closed down the building, and Miep's trying to tell us!

MR FRANK	She'd never telephone us.	20
DUSSEL	*(Frantic.)* Mr Frank, answer that! I beg you, answer it!	
MR FRANK	No.	
MR VAN DAAN	Just pick it up and listen. You don't have to speak. Just listen and see if it's Miep.	
DUSSEL	*(Speaking at the same time.)* For God's sake . . . I ask you.	
MR FRANK	No. I've told you, no. I'll do nothing that might let anyone know we're in the building.	
PETER	Mr Frank's right.	
MR VAN DAAN	There's no need to tell us what side you're on.	
MR FRANK	If we wait patiently, quietly, I believe that help will come.	30
	(There is silence for a minute as they all listen to the telephone ringing.)	
DUSSEL	I'm going down. *(He rushes down the steps. MR FRANK tries ineffectually to hold him. DUSSEL runs to the lower door, unbolting it. The telephone stops ringing. DUSSEL bolts the door and comes slowly back up the steps.)* Too late. *(MR FRANK goes to MARGOT in ANNE'S bedroom.)*	
MR VAN DAAN	So we just wait here until we die.	
MRS VAN DAAN	*(Hysterically.)* I can't stand it! I'll kill myself! I'll kill myself!	
MR VAN DAAN	For God's sake, stop it!	40
	(In the distance, a German military band is heard playing a Viennese waltz.)	
MRS VAN DAAN	I think you'd be glad if I did! I think you want me to die!	

a Viennese waltz *A light dance tune, which contrasts both with the musicians playing it (Nazi soldiers) and the tense atmosphere in the attic.*

MR VAN DAAN	Whose fault is it we're here? *(MRS VAN DAAN starts for her room. He follows, talking at her.)* We could've been safe somewhere . . . in America or Switzerland. But no! No! You wouldn't leave when I wanted to. You couldn't leave your things. You couldn't leave your precious furniture.
MRS VAN DAAN	Don't touch me!
	(She hurries up the stairs, followed by MR VAN DAAN. PETER unable to bear it, goes to his room. ANNE looks after him, deeply concerned. DUSSEL returns to his post at the window. Mr FRANK comes back into the main room and takes a book, trying to read. MRS FRANK sits near the sink, starting to peel some potatoes. ANNE quietly goes to PETER'S room, closing the door after her. PETER is lying face down on the cot. ANNE leans over him, holding him in her arms, trying to bring him out of his despair.)
ANNE	Look, Peter, the sky. *(She looks up through the skylight.)* What a lovely, lovely day! Aren't the clouds beautiful? You know what I do when it seems as if I couldn't stand being cooped up for one more minute? I think myself out. I think myself on a walk in the park where I used to go with Pim. Where the jonquils and the crocus and the violets grow down the slopes. You know the most wonderful part about thinking yourself out? You can have it any way you like. You can have roses and violets and chrysanthemums all blooming at the same time . . . It's funny . . . I used to take it all for granted . . . and now I've gone crazy about everything to do with nature. Haven't you?
PETER	I've just gone crazy. I think if something doesn't happen soon . . . if we don't get out of here . . . I can't stand much more of it!

 jonquils and crocus and violets *Spring flowers. Jonquils are like daffodils.*

ANNE	(*Softly.*) I wish you had a religion, Peter.
PETER	No, thanks! Not me!
ANNE	Oh, I don't mean you have to be Orthodox . . . or believe in heaven and hell and purgatory and things . . . I just mean some religion . . . it doesn't matter what. Just to believe in something! When I think of all that's out there . . . the trees . . . and flowers . . . and seagulls . . . when I think of the dearness of you, Peter . . . and the goodness of the people we know . . . Mr Kraler, Miep, Dirk, the vegetable man, all risking their lives for us every day . . . When I think of these good things, I'm not afraid any more . . . I find myself, and God, and I . . .

80

(*PETER interrupts, getting up and walking away.*)

PETER	That's fine! But when I begin to think, I get mad! Look at us, hiding out for two years. Not able to move! Caught here like . . . waiting for them to come and get . . . us . . . and all for what?

90

ANNE	We're not the only people that've had to suffer. There've always been people that've had to . . . sometimes one race . . . sometimes another . . . and yet . . .
PETER	That doesn't make me feel any better!
ANNE	(*Going to him.*) I know it's terrible, trying to have any faith . . . when people are doing such horrible . . . But you know what I sometimes think? I think the world may be going through a phase, the way I was with Mother. It'll pass, maybe not for hundreds of years, but some day . . . I still believe, in spite of everything, that people are really good at heart.

100

PETER	I want to see something now . . . Not a thousand years from now!

(*He goes over, sitting down again on the cot.*)

ANNE	But, Peter, if you'd only look at it as part of a great

pattern . . . that we're just a little minute in the life . . . *(She breaks off.)* Listen to us, going at each other like a couple of stupid grown-ups! Look at the sky now. Isn't it lovely? *(She holds out her hand to him. PETER takes it and rises, standing with her at the window looking out, his arms around her.)* Some day, when we're outside again, I'm going to . . .

(She breaks off as she hears the sound of a car, its brakes squealing as it comes to a sudden stop. The people in the other rooms also become aware of the sound. They listen tensely. Another car roars up to a screeching stop. ANNE and PETER come from PETER'S room. MR and MRS VAN DAAN creep down the stairs. DUSSEL comes out from his room. Everyone is listening, hardly breathing. A doorbell clangs again and again in the building below. MR FRANK starts quietly down the steps to the door. DUSSEL and PETER follow him. The others stand rigid, waiting, terrified.

In a few seconds DUSSEL comes stumbling back up the steps. He shakes off PETER'S help and goes to his room. MR FRANK bolts the door below, and comes slowly back up the steps. Their eyes are all on him as he stands there for a minute. They realise that what they feared has happened. MRS VAN DAAN starts to whimper. MR VAN DAAN puts her gently in a chair, and then hurries off up the stairs to their room to collect their things. PETER goes to comfort his mother. There is a sound of violent pounding on a door below.)

MR FRANK   *(Quietly.)* For the past two years we have lived in fear. Now we can live in hope.

(The pounding below becomes more insistent. There are muffled sounds of voices, shouting commands.)

MEN'S VOICES   Auf machen! Da drinnen! Auf machen! Schnell! Schnell! Schnell! etc., etc.

(The street door below is forced open. We hear the heavy tread of footsteps coming up. MR FRANK gets two school bags from the shelves, and gives one to ANNE and the other to MARGOT. He

goes to get a bag for MRS FRANK. The sound of feet coming up 140
grows louder. PETER comes to ANNE, kissing her good-bye, then
he goes to his room to collect his things. The buzzer of their door
starts to ring. MR FRANK brings MRS FRANK a bag. They stand
together, waiting. We hear the thud of gun butts on the door,
trying to break it down.

ANNE stands, holding her school bag, looking over at her father
and mother with a soft reassuring smile. She is no longer a child,
but a woman with courage to meet whatever lies ahead.

The lights dim out. The curtain falls on the scene. We hear a
mighty crash as the door is shattered. After a second ANNE'S 150
VOICE is heard.)

ANNE'S VOICE   And so it seems our stay here is over. They are waiting for
us now. They've allowed us five minutes to get our things.
We can each take a bag and whatever it will hold of
clothing. Nothing else. So, dear Diary, that means I must
leave you behind, Goodbye for a while. P.S. Please, please,
Miep, or Mr Kraler, or anyone else. If you should find this
diary, will you please keep it safe for me, because some day
I hope . . .

(Her voice stops abruptly. There is silence. After a second the 160
curtain rises.)

Auf machen! . . . *Open up! You inside! Open up! Quickly!* . . .

DISCUSSION: As a class, discuss who you think is trying to
telephone. What are the possibilities? What is most likely?

HOT-SEATING: Hot-seat Anne. Among other things, ask her why she
is always so optimistic.

ACT 2 ❖ SCENE 5

It is again the afternoon in November, 1945. The rooms are as we saw them in the first scene. MR KRALER has joined MIEP and MR FRANK. There are coffee cups on the table. We see a great change in MR FRANK. He is calm now. His bitterness is gone. He slowly turns a few pages of the diary. They are blank.

MR FRANK   No more.

(He closes the diary and puts it down on the couch beside him.)

MIEP   I'd gone to the country to find food. When I got back the block was surrounded by police . . .

MR KRALER   We made it our business to learn how they knew. It was the thief . . . the thief who told them.

(MIEP goes up to the gas burner, bringing back a pot of coffee.)

MR FRANK   *(After a pause.)* It seems strange to say this, that anyone could be happy in a concentration camp. But Anne was happy in the camp in Holland where they first took us. After two years of being shut up in these rooms, she could be out . . . out in the sunshine and the fresh air that she loved.

MIEP   *(Offering the coffee to MR FRANK.)* A little more?

MR FRANK   *(Holding out his cup to hers.)* The news of the war was good. The British and Americans were sweeping through France. We felt sure that they would get to us in time. In September we were told that we were to be shipped to Poland . . . The men to one camp. The women to another. I was sent to

Auschwitz . . . Belsen . . . Buchenwald . . . Mauthausen . . . *Some of the notorious concentration camps in which many Jews died. (See the map on page v.)*

Auschwitz. They went to Belsen. In January we were freed, 20
the few of us who were left. The war wasn't yet over, so it
took us a long time to get home. We'd be sent here and
there behind the lines where we'd be safe. Each time our
train would stop . . . at a siding, or a crossing . . . we'd all
get out and go from group to group . . . Where were you?
Were you at Belsen? At Buchenwald? At Mauthausen? Is it
possible that you knew my wife? Did you ever see my
husband? My son? My daughter? That's how I found out
about my wife's death . . . of Margot, the Van Daans . . .
Dussel. But Anne . . . I still hoped . . . Yesterday I went to 30
Rotterdam. I'd heard of a woman there . . . She'd been in
Belsen with Anne . . . I know now.

*(He picks up the diary again, and turns the pages back to find a
certain passage. As he finds it we hear ANNE'S VOICE.)*

ANNE'S VOICE   In spite of everything, I still believe that people are really
good at heart.

(MR FRANK slowly closes the diary.)

MR FRANK   She puts me to shame.

(They are silent.)

The curtain falls 40

WRITING: Write an article for an underground resistance newspaper
about the arrest and the events leading up to it. Look back at what
you prepared for the first writing activity in Act 1, Scene 2.

WRITING: Complete the character profiles.

WRITING: Look at one of the character profiles that you have written. Imagine
that you are that character and have arrived at a concentration camp. Use the
details in the profile to write a note to someone in an adjoining hut, explaining
who you are and how you have spent the past two years.

Extracts from the Original Diary of Anne Frank

Saturday, 20th June, 1942

I haven't written for a few days, because I wanted first of all to think about my diary. It's an odd idea for someone like me to keep a diary; not only because I have never done so before, but because it seems to me that neither I – nor for that matter anyone else – will be interested in the unbosomings of a thirteen-year old schoolgirl. Still, what does that matter? I want to write, but more than that, I want to bring out all kinds of things that lie buried deep in my heart.

There is a saying that 'paper is more patient than man'; it came back to me on one of my slightly melancholy days, while I sat chin in hand, feeling too bored and limp even to make up my mind whether to go out or to stay at home. Yes, there is no doubt that paper is patient and as I don't intend to show this cardboard-covered notebook, bearing the proud name of 'diary', to anyone, unless I find a real friend, boy or girl, probably nobody cares. And now I come to the root of the matter, the reason for my starting a diary: it is that I have no such real friend.

Let me put it more clearly, since no one will believe that a girl of thirteen feels herself quite alone in the world, nor is it so. I have darling parents and a sister of sixteen. I know about thirty people whom one might call friends – I have strings of boy friends, anxious to catch a glimpse of me and who, failing that, peep at me through mirrors in class. I have relations, aunts and uncles, who are darlings too, a good home, no – I don't seem to lack anything. But it's the same with all my friends, just fun and games, nothing more. I can never bring myself to talk of anything outside the common round. We don't seem to be able to get any closer, that is the root of the trouble. Perhaps I lack confidence, but anyway, there it is, a stubborn fact and I don't seem to be able to do anything about it.

Hence, this diary. In order to enhance in my mind's eye the picture of the friend for whom I have waited so long, I don't want to set down a series of bald facts in a diary like most people do, but I want this diary itself to be my friend, and I shall call my friend Kitty. No one will grasp what I'm talking about if I begin my letters to Kitty just out of the blue, so, albeit unwillingly, I will start by sketching in brief the story of my life.

My father was 36 when he married my mother, who was then 25. My sister Margot was born in 1926 in Frankfort-on-Maine. I followed on 12th June, 1929, and, as we are Jewish, we emigrated to Holland in 1933, where my father was appointed Managing Director of Travies N.V. This firm is in close relationship with the firm of Kolen & co. in the same building, of which my father is a partner.

The rest of our family, however, felt the full impact of Hitler's anti-Jewish laws, so life was filled with anxiety. In 1938, after the pogroms, my two uncles (my mother's brothers) escaped to the U.S.A. My old grandmother came to us, she was then 73. After May, 1940, good times rapidly fled: first the war, then the capitulation, followed by the arrival of the Germans. That is when the sufferings of us Jews really began. Anti-Jewish decrees followed each other in quick succession. Jews must wear a yellow star, Jews must hand in their bicycles, Jews are banned from trams and are forbidden to drive. Jews are only allowed to do their shopping between three and five o'clock and then only in shops which bear the placard 'Jewish shop'. Jews must be indoors by eight o'clock and cannot even sit in their own gardens after that hour. Jews are forbidden to visit theatres, cinemas, and other places of entertainment. Jews my not take part in public sports. Swimming baths, tennis courts, hockey fields, and other sports grounds are all prohibited to them. Jews may not visit Christians. Jews must go to Jewish schools, and many more restrictions of a similar kind.

So we could not do this and were forbidden to do that. But life went on in spite of it all. Jopie used to say to me: 'You're scared to do anything, because it may be forbidden.' Our freedom was strictly limited. Yet things were still bearable.

Granny died in January, 1942; no one will ever know how much she is present in my thoughts and how much I love her still.

In 1934 I went to school at the Montessori Kindergarten and continued there. It was at the end of the school year, I was in form 6B, when I had to say good-bye to Mrs. K. We both wept, it was very sad. In 1941 I went, with my sister Margot, to the Jewish Secondary School, she into the fourth form and I into the first.

So far everything is all right with the four of us and here I come to the present day.

Saturday, 20th June, 1942

Dear Kitty,

I'll start straight away. It is so peaceful at the moment, Mummy and Daddy are out and Margot has gone to play ping-pong with some friends.

I've been playing ping-pong a lot myself lately. We ping-pongers are very partial to an ice-cream, especially in summer when one gets warm at the game, so we usually finish up with a visit to the nearest ice-cream shop, 'Delphi' or 'Oasis', where Jews are allowed. We've given up scrounging for extra pocket money. 'Oasis' is usually full and amongst our large circle of friends we always manage to find some kind-hearted gentleman or boy friend, who presents us with more ice-cream than we could devour in a week.

I expect you will be rather surprised at the fact that I should talk of boy friends at my age. Alas, one simply can't seem to avoid it at our school. As soon as a boy asks if he may cycle home with me and we get into conversation, nine out of ten times I can be sure that he will fall head over heels in love immediately and simply won't allow me out of his sight. After a while it cools down of course, especially as I take little notice of ardent looks and pedal blithely on.

If it gets so far that they begin about 'asking Father' I swerve slightly on my bicycle, my satchel falls, the young man is bound to get off and hand it to me, by which time I have introduced a new topic of conversation.

These are the most innocent types; you get some who blow kisses or try to get hold of your arm, but then they are definitely knocking at the wrong door. I get off my bicycle and refuse to go farther in their company, or I pretend to be insulted and tell them in no uncertain terms to clear off.

There, the foundation of our friendship is laid, till tomorrow!
Yours, Anne

Sunday, 19th March, 1944

Dear Kitty,

Yesterday was a great day for me. I had decided to talk things out with Peter. Just as we were going to sit down to supper I whispered to him, 'Are you going to do shorthand this evening, Peter?' 'No,' was his reply. 'Then I'd just like to talk to you later!' He agreed. After the washing-up, I stood by the window in his parents' room a while for the look of things, but it wasn't long before I went to Peter. He was standing on the left side of the open window, I went and stood on the right side, and we talked. It was much easier to talk beside the open window in semi-darkness than in bright light, and I believe Peter felt the same.

We told each other so much, so very very much, that I can't repeat it all, but it was lovely; the most wonderful evening I have every had in the 'Secret Annexe'. I will just tell you briefly the various things we talked about. First we talked about the quarrels and how I regard them quite differently now, and then about the estrangements between us and our parents.

I told Peter about Mummy and Daddy and Margot, and about myself.

At one moment he asked, 'I suppose you always give each other a good-night kiss, don't you?'

'One? Dozens! Why, don't you?'

'No, I have hardly every kissed anyone.'

'Not even on your birthday?'

'Yes, I have then.'

We talked about how we neither of us confide in our parents, and how his parents would have loved to have his confidence, but that he didn't wish it. How I cry my heart out in bed, and he goes up into the loft and swears. How Margot and I have only really just begun to know each other well, but that, even so, we don't tell each other everything, because we are always together. Over every imaginable thing – oh, he was just as I thought!

Then we talked about 1942, how different we were then. We just don't recognise ourselves as the same people any more. How we simply couldn't bear each other in the beginning. He thought I was much too talkative and unruly, and I soon came to the conclusion that I'd no time for him. I couldn't understand why he didn't flirt with me, but now I'm glad. He also mentioned how much he isolated himself from us all. I said that there was not much difference between my noise and his silence. That I love peace and quiet too, and have nothing for myself alone, except my diary. How glad he is that my parents have children here, and that I'm glad he is here. That I understand his reserve now and his relationship with his parents, and how I would love to be able to help him.

'You always do help me,' he said. 'How?' I asked very surprised. 'By your cheerfulness.' That was certainly the loveliest thing he said. It was wonderful, he must have grown to love me as a friend, and that is enough for the time being. I am grateful and happy, I just can't find the words. I must apologise, Kitty, that my style is not up to standard today.

I have just written down what came into my head. I have the feeling now that Peter and I share a secret. If he looks at me with those eyes that laugh and wink, then it's just as if a little light goes on inside me. I hope it will remain like this and that we may have many, many more glorious times together!

Your grateful, happy Anne

LOOKING BACK AT THE PLAY . . .

1   DISCUSSION: CASTING THE ROLES
In pairs, discuss which film or television actors you would cast in each of the roles, noting down brief reasons to support your choices. Compare your ideas in a class discussion.

2   ARTWORK AND WRITING: DESIGNING A POSTER
Work in pairs on a poster to advertise a stage, television or film version of *The Diary of Anne Frank*. First, discuss as a class the words and images that usually appear on posters of this kind.

3   DISCUSSION AND WRITING: THE CHANGES IN ANNE
In groups of three, look back through the play and note down the many ways in which Anne has changed by the time of her arrest. Use your notes in a class discussion. Then write an essay entitled 'How Anne changes'.

4   DISCUSSION: THE IMPORTANCE OF SOUND EFFECTS
Imagine that you are doing a school production of the play. In pairs, look through it again and list the different sound effects that you will need. Pick five of them and say how they help (for example, to get the atmosphere across, or create suspense.)

5   ARTWORK: KEY MOMENTS
In groups of six, look back through the play and pick a 'key moment' from each scene (leaving out the first scene.) Draw illustrations of each of these moments and write the relevant piece of dialogue underneath. Then put them together to produce a wall-display.

6   WRITING AND ARTWORK: A THEATRE PROGRAMME:
Create a programme for a production of the play in the theatre. Remember to include the

cast that you have decided on, as well a background article on the Jewish persecution under the Nazis.

7   WRITING: THE PLAY'S 'MESSAGES'
As well as telling Anne's story, the play reveals a lot about human beings in general. Write a short essay showing what the play has to say about: the way people get on together; how some people manage to hold on to their hope and optimism no matter what; and how some are prepared to make great sacrifices to help others.

8   ARTWORK AND WRITING: PETER, MR VAN DAAL AND MR DUSSEL:
Look back at the graph you drew to represent Anne's changing feelings in Act 2, scene 3. Draw a similar kind of graph, this time using the y axis to show how much sympathy you feel for one or more of the following characters as the play goes on: Peter; Mr Van Daal; Mr Dussel. Then write a paragraph on each, explaining your feelings.

9   WRITING: ANNE'S EXPERIENCES
Write a few moments of a scene in which Anne is talking to someone in the first concentration camp, in Holland. What does she say about her experiences? How does she try to give hope to the other person?